KEY

FAMILY
LAW

SECOND EDITION

HELEN L. CONWAY

HODDER
EDUCATION
AN HACHETTE UK COMPANY

Orders: please contact Bookpoint Ltd, 130 Milton Park, Abingdon, Oxon OX14 4SB.
Telephone: (44) 01235 827720. Fax: (44) 01235 400454. Lines are open from 9.00 - 5.00,
Monday to Saturday, with a 24 hour message answering service. You can also order through
our website www.hoddereducation.co.uk.

If you have any comments to make about this, or any of our other titles, please send them to
educationenquiries@hodder.co.uk

British Library Cataloguing in Publication Data
A catalogue record for this title is available from the British Library

ISBN: 978 0 340 94028 0

First Edition Published 2004
This Edition Published 2007

Impression number   10 9 8 7 6 5 4 3
Year   2011 2010 2009

Hachette UK's policy is to use papers that are natural, renewable and recyclable pr
made from wood grown in sustainable forests. The logging and manufacturing
expected to conform to the environmental regulations of the country of orig

Typeset by Transet Limited, Coventry, England.
Printed in Great Britain for Hodder Education, an Hachette UK C
338 Euston Road, London NW1 3BH by Cox & Wyman Ltd.

CONTENTS

Preface

The Key Facts series is a practical and complete revision aid that can be used by students of law courses at all levels from A Level to degree and beyond, and in professional and vocational courses. Family law is generally studied only at degree level or above in either postgraduate or on some professional courses, and also on ILEX Part 2 courses.

The Key Facts series is designed to give a clear view of each subject. This will be useful to students when tackling new topics and is invaluable as a revision aid. Most chapters open with an outline in diagram form of the points covered in that chapter. The points are then developed in a structured list form to make learning easier. Supporting cases are given throughout by name and, for some complex areas, facts are given to reinforce the point being made.

The Key Facts series aims to accommodate the syllabus content of most qualifications in a subject area, using many visual learning aids.

The topics covered for family law include all of those contained in mainstream syllabuses. Family law is often seen as a minority subject. In fact it is more relevant to most people's lives than, for example, criminal law, which is a very popular area of study. Anyone who is in a personal relationship or has children will be affected by the laws contained in this book.

The law is stated as I believe it to be on 30th October 2006.

CHAPTER 1

MARRIAGE AND CIVIL PARTNERSHIP

1.1 MARRIAGE

1.1.1 The definition of marriage

1. Marriage is the voluntary union for life of one man and one woman to the exclusion of all others (*Hyde v Hyde* (1866)).

2.

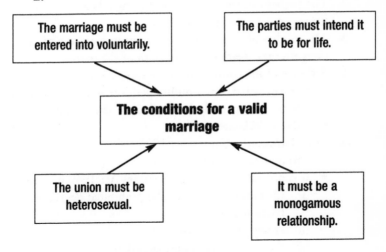

The marriage must be entered into voluntarily.

The parties must intend it to be for life.

The conditions for a valid marriage

The union must be heterosexual.

It must be a monogamous relationship.

3. The Marriage Act 1949 requires:
- for a Church of England wedding – the publications of banns, a license, or a certificate of a superintendent registrar or naval officer;
- for other marriages – a certificate of a superintendent registrar.

4. Marriages can be solemnised in:
- a church or chapel of the Church of England;
- a registered non-conformist church or other building;
- premises approved by the local authority;

- any place if a special licence is obtained.
5. Jews and Quakers may marry according to their own customs with a certificate of a superintendent registrar.
6. Following the Gender Recognition Act 2004 transsexuals may marry according to their 'acquired gender' after issue of a 'gender recognition certificate'.

1.2 NULLITY

1.2.1 Void marriages

1. A void marriage will be treated as never having taken place.
2. The parties can treat it as never having taken place without having to get a decree of nullity.
3. The validity of a marriage can be put in issue at any time even after the death of one or both of the parties.
4. A decree of the court is not necessary to end the marriage as it never existed, but a nullity petition will give access to the court's powers to deal with finance after divorce and will have a declaratory effect.
5. S11 Matrimonial Causes Act 1973 (MCA 1973) sets out the grounds for nullity:
   - It is not valid under the Marriages Act 1949 because:
     (i) the parties are within the prohibited degrees of relationship;
     (ii) either party is under 16;
     (iii) the parties have intermarried.
   - At the time of the marriage either party was already lawfully married.
   - The parties are not male and female. Same sex 'marriages' are not possible (but see Civil partnerships, 1.6 below). Also note that the old cases of *Corbett v Corbett (otherwise Ashley)* [1970] 2 AER 33 and *Bellinger v Bellinger* [2001] 3 FCR 1 deal with transsexual marriages and are superceded by the Gender Recognition Act 2006 which makes marriages of transsexuals in their acquired gender possible.

- The marriage was polygamous, entered into outside England and Wales and one party was domiciled in England and Wales at the time of the marriage. The Private International Law (Miscellaneous Provisions) Act 1995 amended the law so that the marriage is not void simply because it was conducted abroad under a law which allows polygamy, but only if either spouse already had a spouse when married in England and Wales.

6. The prohibited degrees date from 1593 and the common prayer book, but they have been amended over the years, most recently by the Marriage Acts of 1949 and 1960 and the Marriage Enabling Act 1960.

1.2.2 Voidable marriages

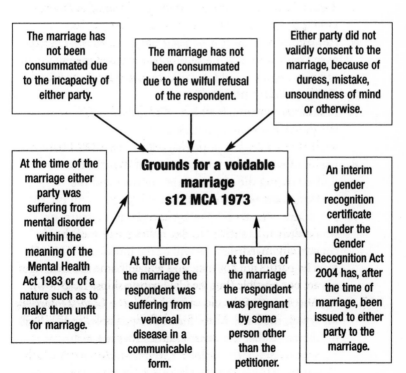

The marriage has not been consummated due to the incapacity of either party.

The marriage has not been consummated due to the wilful refusal of the respondent.

Either party did not validly consent to the marriage, because of duress, mistake, unsoundness of mind or otherwise.

At the time of the marriage either party was suffering from mental disorder within the meaning of the Mental Health Act 1983 or of a nature such as to make them unfit for marriage.

Grounds for a voidable marriage s12 MCA 1973

An interim gender recognition certificate under the Gender Recognition Act 2004 has, after the time of marriage, been issued to either party to the marriage.

At the time of the marriage the respondent was suffering from venereal disease in a communicable form.

At the time of the marriage the respondent was pregnant by some person other than the petitioner.

1. A voidable marriage will be regarded as a valid subsisting marriage until a decree annulling it has been pronounced at the request of one of the spouses.

2. Its validity cannot be challenged after the death of one of the parties.

3. For non-consummation due to incapacity, the incapacity must be incapable of removal by medical or psychological treatment. An inability to conceive or a lack of enjoyment of the intercourse is not sufficient (*Baxter v Baxter* [1947] 2 All ER 43).

4. The incapable party may petition, but a decree will not be given if the other party objects (*Pettit v Pettit* [1962] 3 All ER 37).

5. Wilful refusal to consummate is a 'settled and definite decision come to without just excuse' (*Horton v Horton* [1947] 2 All ER 871).

6. Consummation must have been suggested to the refusing party 'with such tact, persuasion and encouragement as an ordinary spouse would use in such circumstances' (*Baxter v Baxter* [1947] 2 All ER 43).

7. Refusal to go through with a religious ceremony upon which cohabitation is contingent can amount to wilful refusal (*A v J (nullity proceedings)* [1989] 1 FLR 110).

8. For valid consent, the parties must be capable of understanding the nature of the contract and the responsibilities of marriage (*Hill v Hill* [1959] 1 All ER 281).

9. For duress, the test is 'whether the threat, pressure, or whatever it is, is such as to destroy the reality of the consent and overbears the will of the individual' (*H v H* [1953] 2 All ER 1229), or that 'the will of one of the parties thereto has been overborne by genuine and reasonably held fear caused by threat of immediate danger, for which the party is not himself responsible, to life, limb or liberty, so that the constraint destroys the reality of consent to ordinary wedlock' (*Szechter (otherwise Karsov) v Szechter* [1971] P 286, [1970] 3 All ER 905).

10. Arranged marriages are not voidable per se, but forced marriages may constitute duress (*Hirani v Hirani* (1983) 4 FLR 232).

11. Mistakes as to the nature of the ceremony will make a marriage voidable, as will a mistake about the identity of the spouse.

12. However, a misrepresentation about the characteristics of a spouse will not make the marriage voidable as the question is only whether there was reality of consent, not whether it was induced by misrepresentation (*Moss v Moss* [1897] P 263, 66 LJP 154).

13. A sham marriage is still a marriage if the parties knew the effect of the ceremony and willingly entered into to it. This is so even if it was done for nationality or immigration purposes (*Silver (otherwise Kraft) v Silver* [1955] 2 All ER 614; *Puttick v A-G* [1979] 3 All ER 463; *Vervaeke v Smith* [1982] 2 All ER 144).

14. Simply being difficult to live with will not suffice for a petition based on mental disorder. Rather, the ill spouse must suffer from a mental illness under the Mental Health Act 1983 and show that as a result he was incapable of carrying out the ordinary duties and responsibilities of marriage (*Bennett v Bennett* [1969] 1 All ER 53).

15. The illness may be intermittent or continuous.

16. A respondent must show that they did not know about the venereal disease or pregnancy by another man at the time of marriage.

17. Save for non-consummation cases, the application must be within three years of the marriage unless leave is given because of the mental illness suffered by the petitioner.

18. In all cases there is a bar to a decree if the petitioner knew he could have the marriage voided but led the respondent to believe he would not do so and it would be unjust to the respondent to grant the decree.

19. The court cannot grant a decree of nullity based on the granting of an interim gender recognition certificate unless

the proceedings are instituted within the period of six months from the date of issue of that certificate. When granting a decree on this ground the court will then grant a full gender recognition certificate as well.

1.2.3 Jurisdiction in nullity cases

The court may hear a nullity petition if:

- the court has jurisdiction under Council Regulation EC 1347/2001; or
- no court has jurisdiction under that regulation and either of the parties is domiciled in England or Wales on the date proceedings are begun; or
- one of the parties died before proceedings and at the time of the death either was domiciled or had been habitually resident for one year in England and Wales.

1.3 JUDICIAL SEPARATION

1. Judicial separation is based on the same facts and procedure as divorce but a decree can be presented at any time after the marriage.
2. The courts have jurisdiction where:
   - either of the parties are domiciled in England and Wales at the time of the petition;
   - either of the parties were habitually resident in England and Wales for one year before the date of the petition.
3. Irretrievable breakdown is not required for legal separation.
4. After the decree it is no longer obligatory for the parties to live together.
5. For inheritance purposes the parties are treated as if divorced.
6. A finding of fact on a judicial separation petition can be used as proof of facts on a subsequent divorce.

1.4 DIVORCE

1.4.1 Conditions for divorce

1. The parties must have been married for at least a year before a petition may be issued, but a petition may be based on events that happened within the first year of marriage.
2. The courts have jurisdiction where:
   - the court has jurisdiction under Council Regulation EC 1347/2000; or
   - no court has jurisdiction under that regulation and either party is domiciled in England or Wales on the date proceedings begin.
3. The petition is based on the sole ground of irretrievable breakdown, which must be proved by one of five facts in s1 MCA 1973.

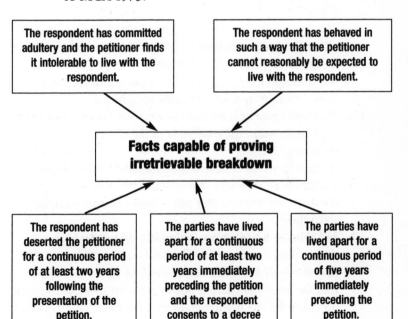

4. Adultery is defined as 'voluntary sexual intercourse between a man and a woman who are not married to each other but one of whom at least is a married person' (*Clarkson v Clarkson* (1930) 143 LT 775, 46 TLR 623).

5. The petitioner cannot rely on adultery if they live with their spouse for six months in total after finding out about it, but any lesser time is ignored.

6. In unreasonable behaviour petitions no account is taken of less than six months cohabitation after events complained of. The court looks at the effect of the conduct on the Petitioner with regard to the history of the marriage (*Buffery v Buffery* [1988] FCR 465, [1988] 2 FLR 365).

7. For a continuous period of desertion, up to six months of cohabitation can be ignored but such ignored time does not count towards the required two-year period.

8. Parties will be taken to be living apart if they do not live in the same household (*Mouncer v Mouncer* [1972] 1 All ER 289).

9. Two households can be established in the same house where the parties establish individual living arrangements.

10. A separation involves some decision to leave the relationship of marriage, not just a physical separation brought about by work or family obligations.

11. Although consent is needed for a divorce based on two years' separation, the consent is to the divorce not the separation itself.

12. If the respondent is misled (intentionally or not) about any matter which they take into account when giving their consent, a decree nisi (but not a decree absolute) can be rescinded.

13. In a divorce based on separation, the respondent can ask the court to consider their financial position. The court may then not make the decree absolute until it is satisfied that the petitioner should not be required to make financial provision for the petitioner, or that the financial provision which has been made is just and fair or the best that can be achieved in the circumstances.

14. If there are circumstances making it desirable that the decree absolute is granted without delay, the court may accept an undertaking from the respondent to make satisfactory financial provision for the petitioner.

15. A respondent to a divorce on five years' separation can oppose the grant of a decree nisi of divorce on the ground that dissolution of the marriage will result in grave financial or other hardship to him and that it would in all the circumstances be wrong to dissolve the marriage (see *K v K (financial provision)* [1996] 3 FCR 158 and *Banik v Banik* [1973] 3 All ER 4).

1.4.2 Procedure for a divorce/judicial separation

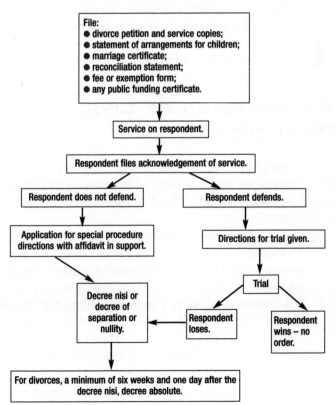

1.4.3 Delaying of civil divorce for a religious divorce

The Divorce (Religious Marriages) Act 2003 inserted s10A into the MCA 1973, which allows the court to delay a decree absolute until the parties have gone through the steps required for a religious divorce according to their faith.

1.5 PRESUMPTION OF DEATH

1. Anyone with reasonable grounds to show their spouse is dead may ask the court for a decree of presumption of death and dissolution of marriage (s19 MCA 1973).
2. If the spouse has been continually absent from the petitioner for seven years, and the petitioner has no reason to believe that the other party has been living within that time, this constitutes evidence that the spouse is dead until the contrary is proved.

1.6 FORMATION OF CIVIL PARTNERSHIPS

1. A civil partnership is a relationship between two people of the same sex which is formed when they register as civil partners of each other (s1 Civil Partnership Act 2004 (CPA)).
2. It ends only on death, dissolution or annulment.
3. To form a civil partnership the partners must sign a 'civil partnership document' in the presence of two witnesses. No religious element to this ceremony is possible and the ceremony may not be in a religious building (s2 CPA 2004).

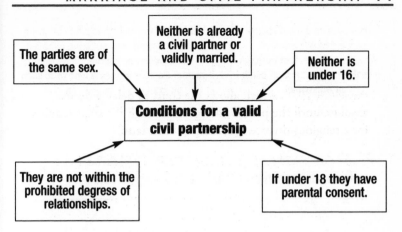

1.7 NULLITY AND CIVIL PARTNERSHIPS

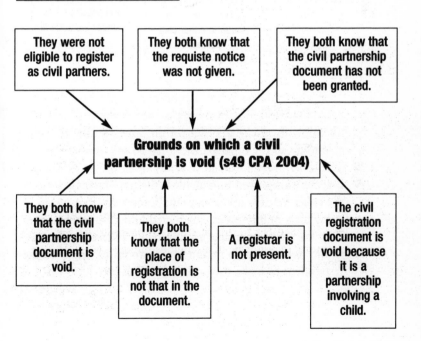

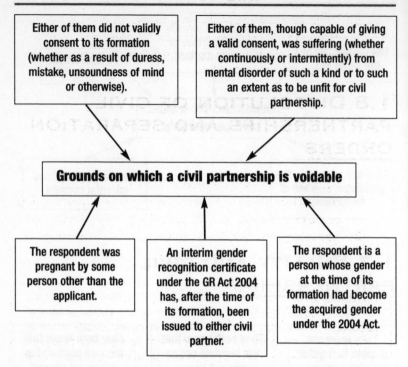

Either of them did not validly consent to its formation (whether as a result of duress, mistake, unsoundness of mind or otherwise).

Either of them, though capable of giving a valid consent, was suffering (whether continuously or intermittently) from mental disorder of such a kind or to such an extent as to be unfit for civil partnership.

Grounds on which a civil partnership is voidable

The respondent was pregnant by some person other than the applicant.

An interim gender recognition certificate under the GR Act 2004 has, after the time of its formation, been issued to either civil partner.

The respondent is a person whose gender at the time of its formation had become the acquired gender under the 2004 Act.

1. Every nullity order is first a conditional order and then made final no less than six weeks later. If the applicant does not apply for the final order within three months of being able to do so the other partner may do so.
2. The court must not make a nullity order on the grounds that the partnership is voidable if the respondent satisfies the court that the applicant, with knowledge that he could apply for a nullity order, conducted himself in such a way as to lead the respondent to reasonably believe that he would not seek to do so and that it would be unjust to the respondent to make the order (s51 CPA 2004).

3. With the exception of the ground that an interim certificate has been issued, the proceedings must be issued within three years of the relationship or leave must be given to issue (s51 CPA 2004).

1.8 DISSOLUTION OF CIVIL PARTNERSHIPS AND SEPARATION ORDERS

1. No application for a dissolution order may be made to the court before the end of the period of one year from the date of the formation of the civil partnership (s41 CPA 2004).
2. The sole ground for dissolution is that the partnership has broken down irretrievably as proven by four set facts.

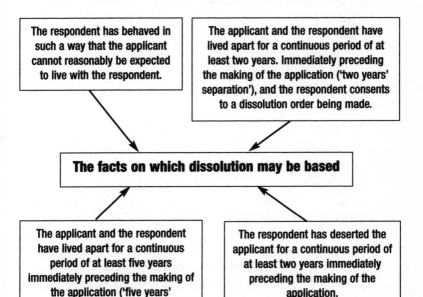

The respondent has behaved in such a way that the applicant cannot reasonably be expected to live with the respondent.

The applicant and the respondent have lived apart for a continuous period of at least two years. Immediately preceding the making of the application ('two years' separation'), and the respondent consents to a dissolution order being made.

The facts on which dissolution may be based

The applicant and the respondent have lived apart for a continuous period of at least five years immediately preceding the making of the application ('five years' seperation').

The respondent has deserted the applicant for a continuous period of at least two years immediately preceding the making of the application.

3. The same facts may lead to a separation order which is available in the first year of the partnership.

4. When calculating the length of time of a separation or a desertion no account is taken of time the partners live together for up to six months in that period but the cohabitation time does not count towards the length of the separation/desertion.

5. The same provisions for protection of a respondent on a five year separation and the same definitions and case law on divorce will apply to civil partnerships.

1.9 THE EFFECT OF CIVIL PARTNERSHIPS

1. Objections from religious groupings influenced the political decision to prevent same sex couples from having a marriage. However, wide amending of legislation has ensured that the effect of a civil partnership is to endow on the participants the same legal status as spouses.

CHAPTER 2
FAMILY LAW ACT 1996, PT IV

2.1 DEFINITION OF DOMESTIC VIOLENCE

1. The Family Law Act 1996 (FLA 1996) does not refer to domestic violence, but to the concepts of 'molestation' and 'harm'.
2. The courts have accepted the dictionary definition of molestation, which is 'to cause trouble, to vex, to annoy, to put to inconvenience' (*Vaughn v Vaughn* (1973)).
3. Harm is defined in s63(1) Family Law Act 1996:
    (i) in relation to an adult: ill-treatment or the impairment of health;
    (ii) for a child: ill-treatment or impairment of health or development (physical, social, emotional or educational);
    (iii) includes sexual abuse and forms of ill-treatment which are not physical.
4. The Adoption and Children Act 2002 adds into that definition harm caused by 'seeing or hearing violence perpetrated upon another' – a recognition of the emotional harm caused to children who witness domestic violence.
5. This is the same definition of harm as is used when making care orders and supervision orders.

2.2 ASSOCIATED PERSONS

1. Previous specialist domestic violence legislation was limited in scope to parties who had been married or heterosexual couples who were living together as man and wife at the time of the last incident complained of. The FLA 1996 as amended widens the scope of protection to 'associated persons'.

Method of association (s62(3) FLA 1996)	Comments
1. Current or former spouses or civil partners.	1. This does not include parties to a void marriage or partnership. There is no minimum length of marriage or any limitation on the time since the divorce.
2. Current or former cohabitees.	2. Following amendments made by the Domestic Violence Crime and Victims Act 2004 cohabitants are defined as a man and woman living together as man and wife or a same sex couple living in an equivalent relationship. It is given a wide purposive definition and may include couples who live between two houses (*G v F (Non-molestation order: Jurisdiction* (2000)).
3. Relatives.	
4. People who live or have lived in the same household otherwise than merely by reason of one of them being the other's employee, tenant, lodger or boarder.	
5. A couple who have agreed to marry each other whether or not that agreement is terminated.	3. This does not include an employee, tenant, boarder or lodger.
6. Persons who have or have had an intimate personal relationship of significant duration (this provision is not yet in force).	4. Relatives are listed in s63(2). They include relatives of a spouse/civil partner or cohabitant.
	5. The engagement must be evidenced in writing, or by an exchange of ring or a ceremony with a witness.
7. Parents of the same child or people who have or have had parental responsibility for the same child.	7. See rules in Chapter 6 on the holding of parental responsibility.
8. Parties to the same family proceedings.	8. Defined s63(1)(2). A body corporate (e.g. a local authority) cannot be associated with an individual.

2.3 RELEVANT CHILDREN

The Act protects both adult applicants and 'any relevant child', which is defined as:

- Any child who is or might reasonably be expected to be living with either party.
- Any child in relation to whom an order under the Adoption and Children Act 2002 or the Children Act 1989 is in question.
- Any other child whose interests are considered relevant. This can include children of a new family (*S v F (Occupation Order)* [2002] 1 FLR 255) or children who visit the home.

2.4 NON-MOLESTATION ORDERS

1. Non-molestation orders are injunctive orders under s42

prohibiting the respondent from molesting the applicant, a relevant child or both.

2. The applicant must be associated with the respondent to make the application, but the relevant child need not be associated with the respondent if the application is made on his behalf by an adult.

3. Children who are associated with the respondent can apply for orders in their own right, but will need leave from the High Court if they are under 16.

4. An application cannot be based on the parties being associated by reason of an engagement if it was broken off more than three years before the application.

5. Applications can be freestanding or applied for within other family proceedings, or the court can make them of its own volition.

6. When making an order, the court must have regard to all the circumstances, including the need to secure the health, safety and wellbeing of the applicant and relevant children.

7. Non-molestation orders can be made for a specified period or until further order of the court.

8. If an order is made in other proceedings, it will automatically cease to have effect if the other proceedings are withdrawn.

9. The usual wording of an order is that the respondent is 'not to harass, pester or otherwise molest, not to use or threaten violence against [the applicant]'.

10. The order may also define what is perceived as being molestation in a particular case, for example if the respondent has a tendency to engage in behaviour which is harassing in the circumstances but which could also have an innocent interpretation.

2.5. HOME RIGHTS

1. Home rights apply where one spouse/civil partner is entitled in property law to occupy the matrimonial home

and the other is not. The current provisions in s30 FLA 1996 replace those in the Matrimonial Homes Act 1983. Prior to the CPA 2004 these were known as 'matrimonial home rights'.

2. If not in occupation, the non-entitled spouse/civil partner has the right, with the leave of the court, to enter into and occupy the property.

3. If in occupation the non-entitled spouse/civil partner has the right not to be evicted or excluded except by an occupation order.

4. The rights end on the death of one spouse/civil partner or a decree absolute, but can be extended beyond the decree absolute by order of the court.

5. The rights operate as an equitable charge on the property and a notice can be registered at the Land Registry.

2.6 OCCUPATION ORDERS

2.6.1 Introduction

1. Occupation orders deal with the future occupation of a shared home. Not all associated persons may apply – provisions are limited to those who have legal rights to occupy the property or who are or were either married or in a civil partnership or cohabitants.

2. However, those categories of applicants are treated differently because of political considerations at the time of the Act. It was passed by a Conservative Government concerned with family values and anxious not to introduce a form of ancillary relief 'by the back door' for non-spouses.

2.6.2 Initial requirements

1. In each category the applicant and respondent must be associated persons.

2. The property to be the subject of the order must have been occupied as their joint home or acquired with the intention that they should live there together.

3. Orders can be made without occurrences of previous violence if the circumstances justify it (*S v F (Occupation Order)* [2000] 1 FLR 255).

4. Occupation orders are draconian orders and require exceptional circumstances (*G v G (Occupation Order: Conduct)* [2000] 2 FLR 533).

2.6.3 Applicants entitled to occupy the property or having home rights (s33)

1. Under s33 the court order may:
   - enforce the applicant's right to remain in the property;
   - require the respondent to allow the applicant to remain in occupation;
   - regulate the occupation of the home;
   - prohibit, suspend or restrict the respondent's right to occupy;
   - restrict or terminate the respondent's home rights;
   - require the respondent to leave the home or part of it;
   - exclude the respondent from a defined area around the home.

2. The first test the court must consider is the significant harm test: if no order is made, will the applicant or a child suffer significant harm attributable to the conduct of the respondent which is greater than the harm the respondent or a child would suffer if the order was made? If this test is passed, the court must make an order (*Chalmers v Johns* [1999] 1 FLR 392 and *B v B (Occupation Order)* [1999] Fam Law 208).

3. If that test is not passed, the court exercises its discretion and must consider:
   - the housing needs and housing resources of each of the parties and of any relevant child;

- the financial resources of each of the parties;
- the likely effect of any order, or of any decision by the court not to make an order, on the health, safety or well-being of the parties and of any relevant child; and
- the conduct of the parties in relation to each other and otherwise.

4. The order may be made for a specified period, until the occurrence of a specified event or until further order.

2.6.4 Applicant is a former spouse/civil partner with no right to occupy the property (s35)

An order for an applicant not in occupation must include provisions:
- giving her the right to enter into and occupy the house for a specified period;
- requiring the respondent to permit exercise of these rights.

An order for an applicant not in occupation must include provisions:
- giving her the right not to be evicted without court order;
- providing a prohibition on the respondent evicting or excluding the applicant.

Compulsory orders

Optional orders

Orders may also:
- regulate the occupation of the home;
- prohibit, suspend or restrict the respondent's right to occupy;
- require the respondent to leave;
- exclude the respondent from a defined area in which the dwelling-house is included.

1. The test is firstly the significant harm test, then discretion looking at:
   - the housing needs and housing resources of each of the parties and of any relevant child;
   - the financial resources of each of the parties;
   - the likely effect of any order, or of any decision by the court not to exercise its powers on the health, safety or wellbeing of the parties and of any relevant child;
   - the conduct of the parties in relation to each other and otherwise;
   - the length of time that has elapsed since the parties ceased to live together;
   - the length of time that has elapsed since the marriage was dissolved or annulled;
   - the existence of any pending proceedings between the parties for property adjustment orders (under Sched 1, Children Act 1989) or relating to the legal or beneficial ownership of the dwelling-house.
2. The order may last for six months, with any number of extensions of up to six months.

2.6.5 Applicant is a cohabitant or former cohabitant with no existing right to occupy, but the respondent does have a right (s36)

1. The same compulsory orders must be made as for a spouse/civil partner with no rights to occupy in property law.
2. The optional orders may:
   - regulate the occupation of the home;
   - prohibit, suspend, restrict the respondent's right to occupy the home;
   - require the respondent to leave the home;
   - exclude the respondent from an area around the home.
3. The only test to be applied is the court's discretion. The relevant factors it must consider are:
   - the housing needs and resources of the parties;

- the parties' financial resources;
- the likely effect of any order or of not making an order, on the health, safety or wellbeing of the parties;
- the parties' conduct to each other and otherwise;
- the nature of the parties' relationship and in particular the level of commitment involved in it;
- the length of time the parties have been living together as husband and wife;
- whether there are any children for whom they have parental responsibility;
- the length of time since they lived together;
- any pending proceedings for financial relief under the Children Act 1989 or in relation to the ownership of the house. For the optional orders the court must also consider the likelihood of significant harm in the future.

4. The order may last six months, with one extension of up to six months.

2.6.6 Applications where neither spouse/civil partner is entitled to occupy the house (s37)

1. This section may apply, for example, where a couple live with their parents or with friends. Orders may:
   - require the respondent to let the applicant enter and remain in the home;
   - regulate the occupation of the home;
   - require the respondent to leave the home, or a part of it;
   - exclude the respondent from a defined area around the home.

2. The court must take into account the same significant harm test, then the same discretion factors as in paragraph 2.6.3.

3. These orders are not enforceable as against the owners of the property, only the respondent.

4. The order may last for six months, with any number of extensions up to six months.

2.6.7 Neither cohabitant or former cohabitant entitled to occupy (s38)

1. The possible orders are the same as for spouses who are not entitled to occupy.
2. The test, however, is the use of the court's discretion only and the relevant factors are:
   - the housing needs and resources of the parties;
   - the financial resources of the parties;
   - the likely effect of making an order or not making an order on the health, safety and wellbeing of a party or relevant child;
   - the conduct of the parties towards each other and otherwise;
   - the likelihood of significant harm in the future.

   The order may last for six months, with one extension of up to six months.

2.6.8 General pattern

1. The significant harm test only ever applies if the applicant has property rights or has married the respondent.
2. The order can only ever be for an immediately open-ended period if the applicant has property rights.
3. Spouses/civil partners without property rights can, in effect, achieve an open-ended order but must renew their applications every six months.
4. Cohabitants without property rights can only ever achieve an order for a maximum of 12 months.

2.7 POWERS OF ARREST

1. The court must make a power of arrest if there has been a use or threat of violence against the applicant or a relevant child *unless* the court is satisfied that the applicant will be adequately satisfied without one.

2. The power allows a constable to arrest without a warrant anyone he has reasonable grounds to suspect is in breach of the order.

3. The arrested person must be brought before the court within 24 hours.

4. If no power is attached but the order is breached, an application must be made for a warrant of arrest.

5. Prison is not the automatic consequence of a breach (*N v R (non-molestation order: breach)*, *The Times*, Tuesday September 1st 1998) but neither is there an assumption that the first breach will lead to a suspended sentence. The sentence will have to consider any parallel criminal proceedings to avoid the same punishment being imposed twice to achieve the same purpose (*Hale v Tanner* [2000] 2 FLR 879).

6. The court can remand in custody or on bail, can sentence to a fine or a period of imprisonment, and can make hospital orders.

7. The arrested person may be prosecuted for the same event that caused him to be arrested (*Director of Public Prosecutions v Tweddle* [2002] 2 FLR 40).

8. If implemented s10 Domestic Violence Crime and Victims Act 2004 will remove the abilty to place powers of arrest onto non-molestation orders (retaining them for occupation orders) and will instead make common assault an arrestable offence, thus pushing the enforcement into the criminal rather than the civil courts.

2.8 UNDERTAKINGS

1. The court may accept an undertaking in lieu of an order. If the court would otherwise have imposed a power of arrest, it should not accept an undertaking unless it believes that the applicant will be adequately protected without one.

2. No power of arrest can be attached to an undertaking, but it is enforceable as if it is an order of the court.

2.9 ADDITIONAL ORDERS (s40 FLA 1996)

An order imposing obligations on either party as to the repair and maintenance of the property, discharge of rent and other outgoings.	An order obliging one occupying party to make periodic payments to the other in respect of the accommodation if the other party is entitled to occupy the home.

ADDITIONAL ORDERS
(inserted in occupation orders)

An order granting either party possession or use of furniture or other contents.	An order that either party should take reasonable care of any furniture or other contents.	An order requiring either party to take reasonable steps to keep the dwelling house and contents secure.

Additional orders which require the payment of money are unenforceable since the FLA 1996 was not made an exception to s4 Debtors Act 1869, which prevents imprisonment for failure to pay money (*Nwogbe v Nwogbe* [2000] 3 FCR 234).

2.10 EXCLUSION REQUIREMENTS

1. Sched 6 FLA 1996 makes these available alongside emergency protection orders and interim care orders.
2. Orders are made against a 'relevant person' (person accused of harming a child or being a risk to a child) who need not be a party.
3. Possible orders:
   - requiring the relevant person to leave the dwelling-house in which he or she is living with a child;
   - preventing the relevant person from entering a dwelling-house in which a child resides;

- excluding the relevant person from entering an area in which the dwelling-house in which the child resides is situated.

4. There must be a person remaining in the home (not necessarily a parent) who is able to give the child such care as it would be reasonable to expect a parent to give them. That person must consent to the order in writing.

5. If being used with an interim care order the test is: if the order is made, would the child cease to suffer harm or cease to be likely to suffer harm.

6. The requirement can be for a shorter period than the interim care order and can be extended on renewals of interim care orders.

7. If being used with an emergency protection order the test is: if the relevant person were excluded, would the child then not be likely to suffer significant harm if he is not removed from his home or if he does not stay in his accommodation, *or* would the frustration of enquiries cease if the relevant person were excluded?

8. Orders lapse if the child is removed from the home for more than 24 hours.

9. The relevant person may apply to vary or discharge the order and powers of arrest.

2.11 THE PROCEDURE

- The application is made in Form FL401.
- A sworn statement in support accompanies the application.
- If the application is made without notice, the statement must explain why.
- A notice of the return date in Form FL402 (and any without notice order) is served personally on the respondent not less than two days before the hearing.
- After the hearing, any order made is drafted on Form FL403 and must be served personally on the respondent to be effective, unless the court dispenses with personal service.

CHAPTER 3

PROTECTION FROM HARASSMENT ACT

3.1 CRIMINAL OFFENCES

3.1.1 Prohibition of harassment (s1)

1. A person must not pursue a course of conduct:
   - which amounts to harassment of another; and
   - which he knows or ought to know amounts to harassment of the other.
2. This objective test is passed if a reasonable person in possession of the same information would think that the conduct amounted to harassment.
3. S7 provides that harassment includes alarming a person or causing distress to them.
4. A course of conduct must involve conduct on at least two occasions and those acts must be proximate in time (see *Lau v DPP* [2000] 1 FLR 799, in which incidents occurring four months apart were deemed insufficient), and *R v Hills* [2001] 1 FCR 569 in which the court held that there must be cogent linking evidence between the events).
5. This Act can be used to protect anyone including persons associated for the FLA 1996 (*Pratt v DPP* [2001] EWHC Admin 483, (2001) 165 JP 800 – two incidents between husband and wife three months apart – borderline case).
6. Conduct cannot constitute harassment if:
   - it was pursued for the purpose of preventing or detecting crime;
   - it was pursued under any enactment or rule of law or to comply with any condition or requirement imposed by any person under any enactment; or

- in the particular circumstances the pursuit of the course of conduct was reasonable.

7. This offence is punishable on summary conviction only. The maximum punishment is six months imprisonment, or a level five fine, or both.

3.1.2 Putting people in fear of violence (s4)

1. It is an offence to cause another to fear, on at least two occasions, that violence will be used against him.

2. The alleged offender must either actually know that his course of conduct will cause the other so to fear on each of those occasions, or his conduct is such that he ought to know.

3. This offence is punishable as an either/or offence.
   - On indictment, the maximum punishment is five years imprisonment, or a fine, or both.
   - On summary conviction the maximum sentence is six months imprisonment, or level five fine, or both.

4. The same defences as s1 are available.

3.1.3 Restraining orders

1. After a conviction or acquittal the court may make an order restraining the defendant from further conduct which amounts to harassment or will cause a fear of violence, for the purpose of protecting the victim of the offence or any other person mentioned in the order.

2. There are no restrictions on what type of behaviour is restrained.

3. The order can have effect for a specified period or until a further order of the court.

4. A breach of a restraining order without a reasonable excuse is a further criminal offence.

5. On indictment, the sentence for such a breach is a maximum of five years and/or a fine.

On summary conviction the maximum is six months
and/or fine at statutory maximum.

6. Persons to be protected by the order must be specifically
named (*R v Mann* (2000) 144 Sol Jo LB 150).

3.1.4 Non-implemented provisions (ss3(3) to (9))

Provisions allowing the court to grant a warrant of arrest on
breach of an injunction or making the breach of a civil order a
criminal offence remain unimplemented.

3.2 CIVIL REMEDIES

1. S3 creates a tort of harassment.

2. Damages (for anxiety and/or financial loss) and
interlocutory injunctions are therefore available for an
actual or apprehended breach of s1. In *Gina Satvir Singh v
(1) Prithvipal Singh Bhakar (2) Dalbir Kaur Bhakar* (2006)
LTL 11/8/2006 (Unreported elsewhere) Document No.:
Case Law – AC0111609 a young Sikh bride who was
controlled and harassed by her mother-in law obtained
damages of £35,000 for the psychiatric damage suffered.

3. The limitation period is six years, although for an
injunction some likelihood of repetition of the behaviour
would in practice be required by the court.

CHAPTER 4

CHILDREN'S RIGHTS

4.1 THE UNITED NATIONS CONVENTION ON THE RIGHTS OF THE CHILD

1. The Convention transforms into legal obligations the affirmations on the Declaration of the Rights of the Child, which was adopted by the general assembly of the United Nations in 1959.
2. The Convention was ratified by the UK in 1991 but was taken into account when the Children Act 1989 was drafted.
3. It is monitored by the Committee on the Rights of the Child, which makes suggestions and recommendations to governments and the general assembly on how the convention obligations can be met.

4.1.1 Definition of child

For the purposes of the UN Convention a child means, 'every human being below the age of 18 years unless, under the law applicable to the child, majority is attained earlier'.
1. The preamble to the Convention talks about the protection of the child before and after birth, but the UK Government entered a reservation limiting the application of the convention to children born alive.
2. This means the Convention does not, in the UK, give the right to life for a foetus.
3. Fathers have no right to act as advocate for the foetus, because the foetus is regarded as not having individual rights (*Paton v Trustees of BPAS* [1979] 2 QB 276).

4.1.2 The main rights given by the Convention

- **Article 2** – all the rights apply to all children, without discrimination on the basis of their race, colour, sex, language, religious, political or other opinion, national or social origin, property, disability, birth or other status.
- **Article 3** – the best interest of the child shall be a primary consideration. The state is to provide adequate care when the family fails to do so.
- **Article 6** – every child has an inherent right to life.
- **Article 7** – every child has a right to a name from birth and to have a nationality.
- **Article 9** – a child has a right to live with his or her parents unless that is incompatible with his or her best interest, and the right to maintain contact with both parents if separated from them.
- **Article 12** – the child has a right to express an opinion and have that opinion taken into account in accordance with his age and maturity.
- **Article 13** – the child has a right to obtain and make known information and to express his or her views.
- **Article 15** – children have a right to free association with others.
- **Article 16** – they have a right to protection from interference with privacy, family, home and correspondence, and from libel and slander.
- **Article 18** – both parents have joint responsibility in bringing up their children and the state should support them in this task.
- **Article 19** – the state has an obligation to protect children from all forms of maltreatment.
- **Article 20** – the state has an obligation to provide special protection for children deprived of their family environment and to ensure an alternative family carer for them, taking into account their cultural background.

- **Article 21** – adoption shall only be carried out in the best interest of the child.
- **Article 22** – special protection is to be given to refugee children.
- **Article 23** – handicapped children are to receive special care, education and training to help them achieve the greatest possible self-reliance.
- **Article 27** – children have a right to an adequate standard of living.
- **Article 28–29** – they have a right to education and at least primary education should be free. Such education should be directed at developing the child's personality and talents, preparing the child for active life as an adult.
- **Article 30** – children of minority communities and indigenous peoples have a right to enjoy their own culture, religion and language.
- **Article 31** – children have a right to leisure, play and participation in cultural activities.
- **Article 32** – states must protect children from work which is a threat to their health, education or development.
- **Article 33–36** – children have the right to be protected from drugs, sexual exploitation and abuse, trafficking and abduction and other forms of exploitation.
- **Article 37** – no child shall be subjected to torture, cruel treatment, capital punishment, life imprisonment or unlawful deprivation of liberty.
- **Article 40** – child offenders have a right to due process of law.

4.2 THE EUROPEAN CONVENTION ON HUMAN RIGHTS

4.2.1 Introduction

1. The Human Rights Act 1998 (HRA 1998) incorporated, indirectly, the European Convention For the Protection of

Fundamental Freedoms and Human Rights 1950 (ECHR) into UK law by requiring courts to interpret domestic law in a manner which is compatible with the Convention.

2. Accordingly, 'human rights' issues may be raised by parties within all family proceedings.

3. The domestic courts are not now bound by precedent created before the HRA 1998, but may reinterpret old law to ensure it is now compatible with the Convention.

4. As an alternative, individuals who believe that their human rights have been breached by a public authority which has acted in a way incompatible with the Convention may sue under s7 and s8 of the HRA 1998.

Article 3
No one shall be subjected to torture or inhuman or degrading treatment or punishment.

Article 6
In the determination of his civil rights and obligations ... everyone is entitled to a fair and public hearing within a reasonable time by an independent and impartial tribunal established by law. Judgement shall be pronounced publicly but the press and public may be excluded from all or part of the trial ... where the interest of juveniles or the protection of the private life of the parties so require.

Relevant ECHR articles

Article 8
Everyone has the right to respect for his private and family life, his home and his correspondence. There shall be no interference with this right except such as is in accordance with the law and is necessary in a democratic society in the interest of national security, public safety or the economic wellbeing of the country, for the prevention of disorder or crime, for the protection of health or morals, or for the protection of the rights and freedoms of others.

Article 12
Men and women of marriageable age have the right to marry and to found a family according to the national laws governing the exercise of this right.

Article 14
The enjoyments of the rights and freedoms set out in this convention shall be secured without discrimination on any ground, such as sex, race, colour, language, religion, political or other opinion, national or social origin, association with a national minority, property, birth or other status.

4.2.2 Freestanding human rights applications in family cases

1. Freestanding applications against a public authority involve a more detailed investigation of the balancing exercise undertaken in the decision-making process than the alternative remedy of judicial review (*R (Daly) v Secretary of State for the Home Department* [2001] 2 AC 532, [2001] UKHRR 887).

2. In HRA 1998 applications to the court must assess whether:
   - an article of the Convention is engaged;
   - it has been interfered with;
   - the interference is in accordance with the law, and that law is reasonably foreseeable and accessible;
   - the interference is in pursuit of a legitimate aim;
   - that interference is 'necessary in a democratic society'. This means it must correspond to a 'pressing social need' and is a 'proportionate' response to the problem. The more serious the intervention the more compelling must be the justification (*C v Bury MBC* [2002] 2 FLR 868).

3. If there are existing care proceedings, human rights issues should be raised within those proceedings as all tiers of the family court system have jurisdiction under HRA 1998 (*Re L (Care Proceedings: Human Rights Claims)* [2003] Fam Law 466).

4. After care orders are made, the parents and children continue to have a right to respect for their family life. Allegations of interference at this stage can be made as a freestanding civil application, or an application can be made under the CA 1989 and the human rights issues raised in those proceedings (*Re S (minors) (Care order: Implementation of care plan), Re W (minors) (Care order: Adequacy of care plan)* [2002] All ER 192, [2002] 1 FLR 815).

4.2.3 A local authority's failure to protect children

1. A public authority has a positive duty to ensure that the rights of individuals are secured, as well as ensuring that its own acts were not incompatible with the convention (*F v Lambeth London Borough Council* [2002] 1 FLR 217).
2. The European Court has held that the failure of a local authority to take into care four children who then suffered serious neglect and abuse amounted to inhuman and degrading treatment (*Z v UK* [2001] 2 FLR 612).
3. Similarly, leaving children in a home where a convicted abuser was known to reside and who subsequently abused the children was a breach of Article 3. The local authority should have investigated and taken steps to stop the abuse happening and to manage the case properly (*E and others v United Kingdom* [2003] 1 FLR 348).

4.2.4 Procedural rights

1. The right to respect for family life means that parents must be involved in decision making to a degree which is sufficient to offer adequate procedural protection for their interests (*W v United Kingdom* (1988) 10 EHHR 29).
2. The right to a fair trial includes the ability to take issues relating to your civil rights to court, not merely being afforded a fair process when you get there (*Golder v UK* (1975) 1 EHRR 524).
3. Although there may be circumstances in which parents allege breaches of their rights after a care order is made but there is no relevant application available under the CA 1989, this does not make the CA 1989 incompatible with the Convention because the matter can be dealt with by way of freestanding application under s7 and s8 HRA 1998 (*Re S (minors) (Care order: Implementation of care plan), Re W (minors) (Care order: Adequacy of care plan)* [2002] All ER 192, [2002] 1 FLR 815).

4. A fair trial does not just comprise fairness at the judicial stage but fairness throughout the litigation process, and all documents and meetings must be open to all parties (*Re L (Care: assessment: Fair Trial)* [2002] 2 FLR 730).

5. Individuals must be given the opportunity to contest the reliability, relevance or sufficiency of the information being compiled on them (*Venema v The Netherlands* [2003] 1 FLR 552).

6. Procedural safeguards continue after the litigation is over. If there is to be a change in a care plan, parents must be told of the proposed changes and given the opportunity to make representations and to challenge the evidence on which the changes are based. The local authority is under a duty to make full and frank disclosure of all relevant information (*Re G (Care: Challenge to Local Authority's decision)* [2003] 1 FLR 42).

7. Procedural flaws may not be sufficiently severe to affect the outcome of the case and justify a local authority's decision being set aside (*C v Bury MBC* [2002] 2 FLR 868).

8. Unless there are justifiable reasons to the contrary, a father without parental responsibility should be given leave to be joined in applications relating to his child to secure respect for his family life (*Re B* [1999] 2 FLR 408).

9. Other applicants for leave to make applications under s8 CA 1989, such as grandparents, may also have Article 6 and 8 rights, and the minimum essential protection of these rights is that judges must be careful not to dismiss the applications without full inquiry (*Re J (leave to issue application for residence order)* [2003] 1 FLR 114).

4.2.5 Proportionality of response

1. The actions of a local authority must be proportionate to the current risk of harm to the child concerned. Action must not be excessive or arbitrary. The lowest-level protective mechanisms must be used first. So removal of a

child from a mother who was not currently mentally ill and who was in the controlled environment of a hospital was unjustified (*K & T v Finland* [2000] 2 FLR 79).

2. The local authority must look at the type of harm alleged and at the timescale within which it is thought likely that the risk will come to fruition when choosing protective measures (*Re C & B (Children) (Care Order: future harm)* [2000] 2 FCR 614).

3. If a supervision order would work because there was a level of parental cooperation and the risk of harm was at the low end of the spectrum, a care order which gave the local authority parental responsibility when they did not need it would be a disproportionate response (*Re O (Supervision Order)* [2001] 1 FLR 923).

4.2.6 Balancing conflicting human rights

1. It may be necessary and proportionate to interfere with a parent's human rights to protect the human rights of a child, such as where granting a very late application by a father to be joined in proceedings would breach the child's right to a fair trial by causing undue delay (*Re P: Care Proceedings: Father's application to be joined as party)* [2001] 1 FLR 781).

2. In judicial decisions where the Article 8 rights of the parents and those of a child are at stake, the child's rights must be the paramount consideration. If any balancing of rights is necessary, those of the child must prevail (*TP and KM v United Kingdom* [2001] ECHR 2, [2001] 2 FLR 549 and *Yousef v Netherlands* [2003] 1 FLR 210).

CHAPTER 5

INTRODUCTION TO THE CHILDREN ACT 1989

5.1 THE THREE MAIN PRINCIPLES OF THE CA 1989

5.1.1 The welfare principle

1. When a court determines *any* question with respect to (a) the upbringing of a child, or (b) the administration of a child's property or income arising from it, the child's welfare shall be the paramount consideration.

2. The principle does not just apply to applications under CA 1989 but to any decision relating to a child, such as the use of the High Court's inherent jurisdiction. The same test now applies in adoption proceedings.

3. It does not bind parents or institutions who are dealing with children.

4. It does not cover Local Authorities who have duties under Part III of the CA 1989 to all children in their area in general, rather than an individual child whose welfare would be paramount and conflict with those general duties to the others.

5. It does not apply if there is a statutory exclusion – the Adoption Act 1976 and the Matrimonial Causes Act 1973 makes the welfare of children in adoption the court's first consideration, and maintenance is excluded from the definition of 'welfare' by the CA 1989.

6. 'Paramount' means the child's welfare determines the course to be followed. It outweighs any one other consideration or any group of other factors pointing in favour of another party (*J v C* [1970] AC 668).

7. For sibling groups each individual child must be considered separately, but on occasions there will be a conflict. The courts have said that they must choose the 'least worst' solution (*Re D (minors)(Appeals)* [1995] 1 FLR 495) or 'the lesser of the two evils and so [find] the least detrimental alternative' (*Re A (children) (conjoined twins: surgical separation)* [2000] 4 All ER 961).

8. If the parent is also still a child, the welfare test applies to the child about whom the actual decision is being made (*F v Leeds City Council* [1994] 2 FCR 428, [1994] 2 FLR 60).

9. The welfare principle does not apply to questions only indirectly involving a child's upbringing, e.g. applications for leave to apply for an order, blood tests or the exclusion of a child's parent from the home (*S v S, W v Official Solicitor* [1970] 3 All ER 107; *Re A (minors) (Residence Orders: Leave to Apply)* [1992] 3 All ER 872; *Richards v Richards* [1984] 2 All ER 80).

10. Applying the principle does not mean that the court must achieve the ideal outcome for the child which may not be possible, but rather, the court is faced with two less than ideal options. The judge should 'appreciate the factors in each direction and to decide which of the two bad solutions was the least dangerous, having regard to the long-term interests of the children' (*Clarke-Hunt v Newcombe* [1982] 4 FLR 482).

5.1.2 The no-delay principle

1. In any proceedings in which the upbringing of a child arises, the court shall have regard to the general principle that any delay in determining the question is likely to prejudice the welfare of the child.

2. This principle applies to all proceedings, not just Children Act 1989 orders.

3. It leads to the making of timetables in court directions: see Family Proceedings Rules 1991 (FPR 1991), Family Proceedings Courts (Children Act 1989) Rules 1991.

4. A period of purposive delay may be justifiable, for example, to allow the court to have an assessment of the mother or to give a father the opportunity to establish a commitment and attachment to a child (*Re B (a minor) (Contact) (Interim Order)* [1994] 2 FLR 269).

5. In care cases, the no-delay principle is now assisted by the Protocol for the Judicial Case Management of Public Child Law Cases, which sets out maximum timescales for steps in the case. The Presidents Private Law Programme of 24/1/04 is being implemented piecemeal and in varied forms around the country.

5.1.3 The no-order principle

1. Where a court is considering whether or not to make one or more orders under the Children Act 1989, it shall not make the order, or any order unless it is satisfied that doing so would be better than making no order at all.

2. The principle prevents unnecessary orders being made automatically which may increase hostility in the family. It also assists the welfare principle by ensuring orders are not made just because the grounds are satisfied, but only when the child's welfare requires it.

3. If no order is to be made, the application must be dismissed and reasons given for no order being made (*S v R (parental responsibility)* [1993] 1 FCR 331).

4. This principle does not apply to applications for financial provision under Sched 1 Children Act 1989 (*K v H: Financial Provision for a child* [1993] 2 FLR 61).

5. The applicant must show that there is a positive case for an order and that it will lead to an improvement over current arrangements from the child's point of view. The case will be decided on its individual facts and there can be no set

presumptions established that an order will or will not be made (*Re X and Y* [2001] 2 FLR 1156).

6. Lack of a dispute between parents is not fatal in the making of an order, which can be made by consent where the agreement needs the encouragement and support of the court (*S v E (access to child)* [1993] 1 FCR 729), or where the order gives a status that would not otherwise exist *(B v B (a minor) (Residence order)* [1992] 2 FLR 327).

5.2 THE WELFARE CHECKLIST

5.2.1 Application

1. The checklist in s1(3) CA 1989 applies where:
   - the court is considering whether to make, vary, or discharge a s8 order (residence, contact, specific issue, prohibited steps) and the making, variation, or discharge of the order is opposed; or
   - the court is considering making a Part IV order (care, supervision, contact to a child in care, educational supervision order).

2. The checklist contains a list of factors, all of which must be considered by the court in cases where it applies.

3. Even when the checklist is not compulsory (e.g. on applications for parental responsibility orders or for financial provision for a child) the court may use it as an *aide-mémoire* (*Re DB and CB (minors)* [1993] 2 FCR 607).

4. CAFCASS officers are required by rules of court to use the checklist when writing reports (Family Proceedings Rules 1991, r 4.11(1)).

5.2.2 The contents of the checklist

1. The ascertainable wishes and feelings of the child concerned (considered in the light of his age and understanding).

- The child's views are not necessarily decisive, as a child may wish for something contrary to his overall welfare (*Re M (Family Proceedings: Affidavits)* [1995] 2 FLR 100).
- There is no set age at which a child is deemed able to express a view, but children's views do carry more weight as the child gets older (*Re P (minors) (Wardship: Care and Control)* [1992] 2 FCR 681).
- While children should be listened to and consulted, they should not be asked to make decisions which involve them choosing one parent over the other (*Re S (Contact: Children's Views)* [2002] 1 FLR 1156).

2. The child's physical, emotional and educational needs.
- Disadvantages of a material sort relating to the parent's respective standards of living must be of little weight (*Stephenson v Stephenson* [1985] FLR 1140 at 1148).
- The general view is that siblings have an emotional need to be brought up together unless there are strong reasons to the contrary (*C v C (minors) (Custody)* [1988] 2 FLR 291).
- There is a presumption that a child should live with their natural parents unless the child's welfare requires otherwise, for example when a non-parent has cared for a child for so long they have become a 'psychological parent'. The first question is: 'Can a parent offer suitable care for a child?', not: 'Who would be the better carer between a parent and a third party such as an aunt or grandmother?' (*Re W (a minor) (Residence Order)* [1993] 2 FLR 625 at 633).
- The educational needs of a child may include their religious upbringing (e.g. *Re J (child's religious upbringing and circumcision)* [1999] 2 FCR 3).

3. The likely effect on the child of any change in his circumstances.
- The current status quo prevailing in the family carries great weight if it is satisfactory. Disruption is to be

avoided where possible (*Dicocco v Milne* [1982] 4 FLR 247; *S v W* (1981) 11 Fam Law 81).

- The status quo is not just the position immediately before the court hearing. The court will look at the whole family history (*Allington v Allington* [1985] FLR 586).
- Technically, orders do not alter the status quo, but a long interim period may impact on the end result in practice by affecting other checklist items.

4. The child's age, sex, background and any characteristics of his which the court considers relevant.

- There is no presumption of law that a child of any given age is better off with a parent of a certain gender. There is no rule to say that fathers cannot be sole carers for their children (*Re W (a minor) (Residence Order)* [1992] 2 FLR 332).
- Individual cases vary, so there can be no general principle, but the court must consider:
    (i) the capacity of the individual adults concerned to care for the child;
   (ii) if all other factors are balanced it is probably right for a child of tender years to be with their mother;
  (iii) if the child has in fact been brought up by someone else (e.g. the father and his partner) for a long time, what will be the effect of uprooting the child now? (*Re W (a minor) (Custody)* [1982] 4 FLR 492).
- Links with the family's culture and heritage should be preserved where possible (*Re M (Child's Upbringing)* [1996] 2 FCR 473).

5. Any harm which the child has suffered or is at risk of suffering.

- Harm has the same meaning as for care orders and includes ill-treatment, physical, intellectual, sexual and emotional harm and impairment of social or emotional development.

- The Adoption and Children Act 2002 extends the definition of harm to include 'impairment suffered by seeing or hearing the ill-treatment of another' to cover children who witness domestic violence.

- A finding that the child is at risk of harm in the future must be based on proved facts and not simply suspicion or mere doubts. The standard of proof is the 'preponderance of probabilities' (*Re M and R (Child Abuse: Evidence)* [1996] 2 FLR 195).

6. How capable each of the child's parents are, and any other person in relation to whom the court considers the question to be relevant, is of meeting his needs.

   - Capacity may be tested by professional assessments by psychologists, psychiatrists or other agencies.

   - Homosexuality does not preclude being able to meet a child's needs (*B v B (Custody of Children)* [1991] FCR 1). A same sex couple may be seen as a 'a family unit' (*Re D (Contact and PR: Lesbian Mothers and Known Father)* (No 2) [2006] EWHC 2 (Fam))

7. The range of powers available to the court under this Act in the proceedings in question.

CHAPTER 6

PARENTAL RESPONSIBILITY

6.1 DEFINITION

> 'All the rights, duties, powers and responsibilities and authority which by law a parent has in relation to a child and his property.'
> s3(1) CA 1989
>
> 'the modern concept according to which parents are, on a basis of equality between parents and in consultation with their children, given the task to educate, legally represent, maintain etc their children. In order to do so they exercise powers to carry out duties in the interest of the child and not because of an authority which is conferred on them in their own interests.'
> Council of Europe

1. These parental rights derive from parental duty and exist only 'so long as they are needed for the protection of the person and property of the child'. The child becomes more autonomous as they grow older (*Gillick v West Norfolk and Wisbeach Area Health Authority* [1986] AC 112).
2. The fact that a parent does not have parental responsibility for a child does not alter any obligation owed to the child, e.g. a duty to maintain them or a right to inherit from them (s3 CA 1989).
3. More than one person at a time can have parental responsibility for a child (s2(5) CA 1989).
4. Each person with parental responsibility can exercise it independently (s2(7) CA 1989). An exception is a change of the child's surname, which the courts have deemed so important it requires the consent of all with parental responsibility.

5. Parental responsibility cannot be surrendered or transferred but may be delegated to anyone (s9(9) CA 1989). It is not lost with the issue of a gender recognition certificate.

6. Parental responsibility does not affect the day-to-day care of the child but provides status for the holder (*Re S (a minor) (Parental Responsibility)* [1995] 3 FCR 564).

7. Parental responsibility cannot be used in a way which is inconsistent with an order of the court.

8. Parental responsibility exists for the benefit of the child, and UK courts have refused damages to adults for interference with it (*Re S (a minor) (parental rights)* [1993] Fam Law 572).

9. The European Court has declared that states do have a positive duty to ensure that parental rights are upheld, for example, by ensuring enforcement of a contact order given to a father (*Hokkanen v Finland* [1996] 1 FLR 289, 19 EHRR 139).

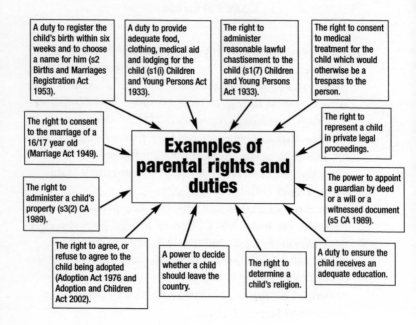

6.2 WHO GETS PARENTAL RESPONSIBILITY?

6.2.1 Married natural parents

1. Mothers automatically obtain parental responsibility on the birth of the child (s2 CA 1989).
2. Fathers who are married to the mother at the time of the birth also obtain parental responsibility automatically (s2 CA 1989).
3. S1 Family Law Reform Act 1987 provides that fathers who subsequently marry the child's mother will automatically get parental responsibility from the date of marriage since the marriage 'legitimises the child'.

6.2.2 Unmarried natural parents

1. Mothers automatically obtain parental responsibility at the time of birth.
2. Unmarried fathers must acquire it by either:
   - obtaining a parental responsibility order from the court (s4(1)(a) CA 1989); or
   - entering into a parental responsibility agreement with the mother (s4(1)(a) CA 1989). This requires a set form, full identification for both parents, a full birth certificate and must be signed before a justice of the peace or a clerk authorised to take oaths, and is then registered at the Principle Registry. A mother may enter into such an agreement even if the court has declined to make a s4 order (*Re X (Parental Responsibility Agreement: Children in Care)* [2000] 1 FLR 517);
   - s111 Adoption and Children Act 2002 created s4(1)(a) CA 1989 – after 1 December 2003 fathers who are named on the birth certificate will automatically get parental responsibility.

3. Denying unmarried fathers parental responsibility automatically is not discrimination under the ECHR because there is an objective and justifiable reason for it, namely the range of relationships between unmarried fathers and their children (*B v UK* [2000] 1 FLR 1).

4. Factors relevant to the making of a parental responsibility order are:
   - the degree of commitment which the father has shown towards the child;
   - the degree of attachment which exists between the father and the child;
   - the reasons the father is applying for the order (*Re H (minors) (adoption: putative father's rights) (No 3)* [1991] 2 All ER 185).

5. The fact that a father meets the above tests does not automatically lead to an order being made, as the overall test remains the welfare of the child (*Re H (Parental Responsibility)* [1998] 1 FLR 855).

6. Parental responsibility is not a reward for a father who has shown commitment (*Re M (handicapped child: parental responsibility)* [2001] 3 FCR 454, [2001] 2 FLR 342).

7. It may be appropriate to give parental responsibility to a father who cannot use it at once to give him standing in future proceedings (*D v Hereford and Worcester County Council* [1991] 2 All ER 177).

8. It should not be refused as a lever to make a father pay child maintenance (*Re H (a minor) (parental responsibility order)* [1996] 3 FCR 49, [1996] 1 FLR 867).

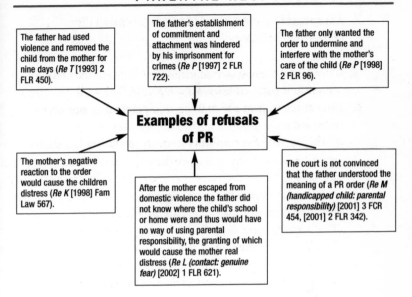

The father had used violence and removed the child from the mother for nine days (*Re T* [1993] 2 FLR 450).

The father's establishment of commitment and attachment was hindered by his imprisonment for crimes (*Re P* [1997] 2 FLR 722).

The father only wanted the order to undermine and interfere with the mother's care of the child (*Re P* [1998] 2 FLR 96).

Examples of refusals of PR

The mother's negative reaction to the order would cause the children distress (*Re K* [1998] Fam Law 567).

After the mother escaped from domestic violence the father did not know where the child's school or home were and thus would have no way of using parental responsibility, the granting of which would cause the mother real distress (*Re L (contact: genuine fear)* [2002] 1 FLR 621).

The court is not convinced that the father understood the meaning of a PR order (*Re M (handicapped child: parental responsibility)* [2001] 3 FCR 454, [2001] 2 FLR 342).

6.2.3 Step-parents

S112 Adoption and Children Act 2002 (A&CA 2002) as amended by the CPA 2004 inserts new s4A into CA 1989, providing that:

- the court can grant a step-parent or civil partner of a natural parent parental responsibility;
- a parent married to the step-parent or in a civil partnership can enter into a parental responsibility agreement with the step-parent/civil partner. If the other natural parent also has parental responsibility they must be a party to the agreement;
- in each of these cases the parental responsibility can be removed by the court.

6.2.4 Alternative acquisition of parental responsibility

1. A father obtaining a residence order for his own child must be given a parental responsibility order under s4 CA 1989.
2. Any other person obtaining a residence order will get parental responsibility for the duration of the order only. Such parental responsibility does not allow the appointment of a guardian or the consenting to an adoption.
3. A person appointed as guardian under s5 CA 1989 acquires parental responsibility when the appointment takes effect. The appointment must be in writing and signed and dated. It takes effect when, after the appointing parent dies, there is no one with parental responsibility, or immediately if the deceased parent had a sole residence order.
4. A guardian:
   - is not a 'liable relative' for benefits law;
   - cannot be made subject to financial orders under the Children Act 1989;
   - does not inherit from a child.
5. A guardian may be appointed by the court if the child has no-one with parental responsibility for him, or if a parent or guardian with a residence order has died while the order is in force.
6. An adoption order confers full, irrevocable parental responsibility on the adopters.
7. A placement order under the Adoption and Children Act 2006 will give parental responsibility to the agency and, after placement, the prospective adopters.
8. A care order enables the local authority to share parental responsibility for the child concerned with those parents who also hold it.
9. A special guardianship order (see below) also confers parental responsibilty.

6.2.5 Parental responsibility and artificial insemination/surrogacy

1. For children born by artificial insemination, s28(2) Human Fertilisation and Embryology Act 1990 (HFEA 1990) provides that for a married couple, where a woman has artificial insemination with donor sperm and the husband agrees to the treatment he will be treated as the father of the child.

2. For an unmarried couple having such treatment, a man who has been provided with treatment services together with the woman will be treated as the father of the child (s28(3) HFEA 1990). Where a couple signed for treatment but then split up before the embryo was planted, the Court of Appeal said that they were not treated together (*Re R (IVF: Paternity of Child)* [2003] 1 FLR 1183).

3. Where an unmarried woman has such treatment alone, the sperm donor is not treated as the father of the child and the child is deemed in law to be fatherless.

4. In a surrogacy agreement, the carrying mother is regarded as the mother of the child and holds parental responsibility for the child until it is removed from her, even if she has no genetic connection to the child (s27 HFEA 1990).

5. Where a married couple use a surrogate and the gamete is supplied by husband or wife or both, a parental order may be made under s30 HFEA 1990. The conditions are that:
   - the application is made within six months of the birth;
   - at the time of the application and the making of the order the child is living with the commissioning parents in the UK, the Channel Islands or the Isle of Man;
   - the husband and wife are both over 18;
   - the biological father of the child, if not the commissioning husband (including the husband of the surrogate mother who would be deemed to be the father under s28), and the surrogate mother agree freely and unconditionally to the order;

- no money or benefit other than expenses reasonably incurred have been made or received unless authorised by the court.

6.3 LOSING PARENTAL RESPONSIBILITY

1. The court may, on the application of the child or anyone with parental responsibility, remove any parental responsibility gained by way of a court order, a birth certificate or a parental agreement.
2. Parental responsibility given with a residence order lapses when the order is revoked.
3. All forms of parental responsibility end upon the making of an adoption order.
4. The new placement orders under A&CA 2002 will not remove the parents' parental responsibility until adoption, but will allow the adoption agency to determine the extent to which parents can use it. This ensures a child always has an adult with responsibility for him, not only an agency.
5. Parents whose children are subject to a care order do not lose their parental responsibility, but the local authority is able to limit its use as the child's welfare requires. Parents cannot be prevented from choosing the child's surname or religion or consenting to (or refusing consent to) an adoption.

6.4 SPECIAL GUARDIANSHIP ORDERS

6.4.1 General information

1. A special guardianship order became available after the implementation of the A&CA 2002 by the creation of a new s14A-G CA 1989.

2. The orders provide a halfway house between residence orders and adoption and are likely to be most used for in-family placements.

6.4.2 Who may apply?

1. Orders may be made to one individual or jointly to married couples.
2. Applicants must be over 18 and cannot be the natural parents.
3. Applicants will need leave unless:
   - they are a guardian;
   - they have a residence order;
   - the child has lived with them for three years;
   - they have the consent of all with a residence order;
   - if the child is in care, the local authority consents;
   - they have fostered the child for at least a year immediately before the application.

6.4.3 The procedure

1. The applicants must give their local authority three months' notice of their intent to apply for an order. Alternatively, the court tells the local authority it is contemplating making an order.
2. The local authority must then investigate the suitability of the applicant and such other matters as will be in regulations, then reports to the court.
3. The court must consider:
   - the making of a contact order;
   - which surname the child should use;
   - leave to remove from the jurisdiction for longer than three months;
   - any directions/conditions to be attached;
   - whether any existing s8 orders should be varied/discharged?

6.4.4 The effect of the order

1. A special guardian is appointed.
2. Parental responsibility is not removed from other people who hold it, but the special guardian obtains parental responsibility and may exercise it to the exclusion of all others except another special guardian.
3. Others with parental responsibility can still use it where the law requires the consent of everyone with parental responsibility to consent/refuse to consent to adoption.
4. No-one can cause the child to be known by a new surname without the consent of all those with parental responsibility or leave of the court.
5. The child cannot be removed from the UK for more than three months without the consent of all those with parental responsibility or leave of the court.
6. Existing care orders and s34 orders are discharged.
7. Support services must be made available to special guardians.

6.5 PARENTAL RESPONSIBILITY IN PRACTICE

6.5.1 Parental responsibility and child discipline

1. Parents have the right to administer 'reasonable lawful chastisement' to a child (s1(7) Children and Young Person Act 1933).
2. Whether punishment is reasonable must be assessed in the light of the reasons for the punishment, the age and development of the child.
3. Punishment must have been imposed 'for good reason' and be 'reasonable' (*R v Hopley* (1860) 175 ER 1027).
4. The powers to chastise a child may be delegated (*Davis v London Borough of Sutton* [1994] 1 FLR 737).

5. Corporal punishment was abolished in all state schools in 1986, and later for all schools by s131 School Standards and Framework Act 1998, following the European decision on *Costello-Roberts v United Kingdom* (1993), *The Independent*, March 26.

6. Over-chastisement may be a breach of the child's human rights if it amounts to inhuman or degrading treatment, e.g. by using a strap (*A v United Kingdom (Human Rights Punishment of child)* [1998] 2 FLR 959).

7. S58 CA 1989 removed the defence of reasonable punishment from certain criminal offences, namely wounding, grievous bodily harm, actual bodily harm and cruelty to persons under 16.

6.5.2 Parental responsibility and education

1. S7 Education Act 1996 requires parents to ensure that a child receives an efficient full-time education suitable to his age, ability and aptitude and any special needs he may have by going to school or in other ways.

2. Parents may be guilty of a criminal offence for failing to conform to this duty.

3. Local authorities may seek attendance orders for the child under s437 Education Act 1996 or Educational Supervision Orders under s36 Children Act 1989.

4. Parents may remove their children from religious education provided by schools and provide alternative tuition.

6.5.3 Parental responsibility and medical treatment

1. It is a parental duty to provide adequate medical care for a child.

2. Failure to do so is an offence under s1 Children and Young Persons Act 1933 if it causes the child unnecessary suffering or injury to health.

3. Health professionals will require parental consent to treat a child unless it is a question of necessity in an emergency.

4. If a parent refuses to give consent, the matter can be decided by the court who will consider the parents' wishes carefully but may override them if the treatment is in the child's welfare (*Re C (a child) (HIV test)* [1999] 2 FLR 1004).

5. There is a strong presumption in favour of treatment which will preserve life, but that may be rebutted, for example where the effect is to prolong great suffering or where the resulting quality of life would not be tolerable to the child (*Re J (a minor) (Wardship: medical treatment)* [1990] 3 All ER 930).

6. Parents do not have the right to insist on treatment which doctors decline to give a child on medical grounds (*Re J (a minor) (medical treatment)* [1992] 4 All ER 614).

7. Blood transfusions refused by Jehovah's Witness parents are frequently authorized by the courts (*Re L (Medical treatment: Gillick competency)* [1998] 2 FLR 810).

8. A child under 16 who has sufficient understanding of the issues may consent to treatment against her parents wishes (*Gillick v West Norfolk and Wisbech Area Health Authority* [1985] 3 All ER 402).

9. However, the court may make an order contrary to the wishes of a 'Gillick competent' child (*Re R (a minor) (wardship: consent to treatment)* [1991] 4 All ER 177).

10. A parent cannot override the consent to treatment of an under-16 'Gillick competent' child, but may still give consent when the same child refuses treatment (*Re W (a minor) (medical treatment)* [1992] 4 All ER 627).

11. S8(1) Family Law Reform Act 1969 allows a 16 year old to consent to surgical, medical or dental treatment against a parents wishes without the Gillick test applying.

12. The Act does not give the child the right to refuse treatment, which right lies with the courts or those with parental responsibility for the child.

13. In all cases where the courts have power to make the
    decision, the wishes and feelings of the child must be
    considered and should be given effect unless the balancing
    exercise when considering the child's welfare points to the
    contrary (*Re S (a minor) (Consent to medical treatment)*
    [1994] 2 FLR 1065).

CHAPTER 7

PRIVATE CHILD LAW

7.1 SECTION 8 ORDERS

Residence order
An order settling the arrangements to be made as to with whom a child is to live.

Contact order
An order requiring the person with whom a child is to live to allow the child to visit or stay with the person named in the order, or for them otherwise to have contact with each other.

SECTION 8 ORDERS

Prohibited steps
An order that no step which could be taken by a parent in meeting his parental responsibility for a child, and which is of a kind specified in the order, shall be taken by any person without the consent of the court.

Specific issue order
An order giving a direction for the purpose of determining a specific question which has arisen, or which may arise, in connection with any aspect of parental responsibility for a child.

1. Section 8 orders can be made in a freestanding application, on an application or of the court's own volition within other family proceedings.

2. The court's power to make orders of its own volition can be exercised in favour of someone who is not even a party, such as foster parents caring for a child in care proceedings (*Gloucestershire County Council v P* [1999] 3 FCR 114, [1999] 2 FLR 6).

7.1.1 Specific issue and prohibited steps

1. Orders must allow or restrict an act which would comprise an exercise of parental responsibility, but the person who is the subject of the order need not have parental responsibility (*Re J (Specific issue order: leave to apply)* [1995] 1 FLR 669; *N v N (jurisdiction: pre-nuptial agreement)* [1999] 2 FLR 745).

2. The inherent jurisdiction of the court should be invoked in preference to a specific issue order to deal with applications to sterilize a child (*Practice Note (Official Solicitor: sterilisation)* [1996] 3 FCR 95, [1996] 2 FLR 111) and for contested circumcision cases.

3. Specific issue is frequently used to obtain permission for change of names of children.

   - A sole holder of parental responsibility has sole rights and duty to register the child's name.
   - Married parents have an equal right to choose a name on the birth of the child.
   - It is not mandatory for the child to use the father's name.
   - If a residence order is in force, the written consent of all those with parental responsibility or leave of the court is needed to change a surname of a child.
   - Otherwise, sole holders of parental responsibility can change a name alone. Fathers without parental responsibility can still apply for a specific issue or prohibited steps order to decide a child's name.
   - Joint holders of parental responsibility must obtain the consent of all those with parental responsibility or the leave of the court. Changing a surname is an exception to the general rule that parental responsibility can be exercised unilaterally. The consent need not be in writing unless a deed poll is used and it can be inferred from a lack of response (*Re T (a minor: change of surname)* [1998] 2 FLR 620; *Dawson v Wearmouth*

[1999] 1 FLR 1167; *Re W, Re A, Re B (change of name)*
[1999] 2 FLR 930; and *Re PC (change of surname)*
[1997] 2 FLR 730).

4. Following the making of a care order, parents retain the right to decide the name their child should use.

5. Points the court will consider on an application are:

- Double-barrelling of names should be more frequently considered as it recognises the importance of both parents. It should not be assumed that fathers need to share the same name as the child in order to retain their relationship with the child (*Re R (surname: using both parents')* [2001] 2 FLR 1358).

- Much less emphasis will be placed on registered first names, and a parent may use whatever first names they like in the home as they do not connote the family to which the child belongs and are thus of less importance (*Re H (Child's name: first Name)* [2002] 1 FLR 973).

- Surnames can denote heritage and culture as well as the family to which the child belongs. The court may allow the informal daily use of one set of names while insisting that the child keeps the other set formally to retain links to their heritage (*Re S (change of names: cultural factors)* [2001] 2 FLR 1005).

- The court may be prepared to consider cultural and religious customs or laws, such as Islamic family law, to determine the appropriate surname for a child living in a minority community (*Re A change of name* [2003] 2 FLR 1).

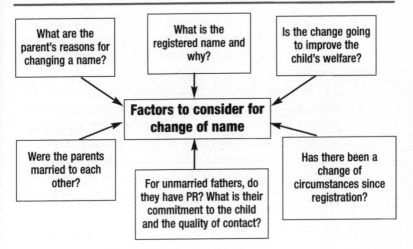

What are the parent's reasons for changing a name?

What is the registered name and why?

Is the change going to improve the child's welfare?

Factors to consider for change of name

Were the parents married to each other?

For unmarried fathers, do they have PR? What is their commitment to the child and the quality of contact?

Has there been a change of circumstances since registration?

7.1.2 Residence orders

1. A shared residence order providing that a child lives with two or more people who do not themselves live together can be made under s11(4) CA 1989 if it meets the welfare of the child. Despite earlier case law, exceptional circumstances are not now needed. The order need only be in the child's interests (*D v D (Shared Residence Order)* [2001] 1 FLR 495).

2. There must be some aspect of shared care for a shared residence order to be made. It is not just about status for the parents. Care need not be equally divided and the parents may live some distance apart (*Re F (Shared residence) CoA July* [2003] Fam Law 543).

3. Courts may be willing to make shared orders to give parental responsibility to a person who is significant in the child's life but who cannot otherwise obtain it, e.g. a step-father or lesbian partner of the mother (*Re H (Shared residence) (parental responsibility)* [1995] 2 FLR 883 and *G v F (Contact and Shared Residence: Applications for Leave)* [1998] 2 FLR 799).

4. S11(5) CA 1989 – if a residence order is made to one of two parents who each have parental responsibility for the child, the residence order lapses if they live together for six months.

5. The order automatically prevents the removal of the child from the jurisdiction without consent of the holder of the order or leave of the court save that the parent with the order may take the child abroad for up to one month.

6. A residence order gives the holder the 'right to determine all matters which arise in the day-to-day management of this child's life' (*Re P (a minor) (parental responsibility order)* [1994] 1 FLR 578).

7. An order – even an interim one – will discharge a care order and confer parental responsibility on the holder.

8. Residence orders may be made without notice to one party but only in compelling circumstances such as to prevent child abduction (*Re B (minors) (Residence Order)* [1992] 3 All ER 867).

7.1.3 Contact orders

1. Contact may be overnight, visiting or indirect (letters, telephone, etc.).

2. The starting point is that contact is good for the child and that they have a right to know both parents. The usual burden of proof is thus reversed and placed on the parent denying contact (*Re F (contact: restraint order)* [1995] 1 FLR 956).

3. Contact should only be denied if there are 'cogent reasons' (*Re H (minors: access)* [1992] 1 FLR 148).

4. A contact order may state that there is to be 'no contact' at all (*Nottingham County Council v P* [1993] 3 AU ER 815).

5. The court will not allow a parent to deprive a child of contact through their own obduracy and will not decline to make an order simply because a party states their intention to disobey it (*Re F (contact: restraint order)* [1995] 1 FLR 956).

6. In cases where no direct contact is to take place, indirect contact is normally desirable (*Re P (Contact: Supervision)* [1996] 2 FLR 314).

7. Indirect contact will usually lead to direct contact unless that is not in the child's welfare. The court should concentrate on the long-term benefits of contact, which will usually outweigh short-term upset to the child (*Re O (Contact: imposition of conditions)* [1996] 1 FCR 317, [1995] 2 FLR 12).

8. Contact orders can be enforced by fine or committal. The first step is to try to get the contact working rather than to punish disobedience (*Thomason v Thomason* [1985] FLR 214).

9. A change of residence from one parent to the other may follow a breach of a contact order, but only if the other parent will allow contact and can offer suitable care to the child.

10. Courts may ultimately commit 'implacably hostile' parents who disobey orders (*A v N (Committal: Refusal of Contact)* (April 1997) Fam Law 233).

11. The court must balance the harm of enforcement against the harm from lack of contact (*Re J (a minor) (contact)* (1994) 1 FLR 729).

12. Where a parent is refusing contact the court should deal with any alleged facts underpinning the refusal. Thereafter, if contact is refused the child may be suffering significant harm and a s37 direction may be appropriate (*Re M (intractable contact dispute: interim care order)* [2003] 2 FLR 636).

7.1.4 Conditions and directions

1. S11(7) CA 1989 allows the court to impose conditions to be complied with by:
    - the person in whose favour the order is made;
    - a parent;

- a person with parental responsibility for a child;
- a person with whom the child is living.

2. A s8 order may also impose directions about how it is to be implemented.

3. A court may use this to require a parent to take positive steps to ensure that contact takes place and is meaningful. Such steps can include sending information about a child to the other parent (*Re O (contact: imposition of conditions)* [1995] 2 FLR 124).

4. Conditions cannot be used to make a carer of a child live at a particular address (*Re E (Residence: Imposition of conditions)* [1997] 2 FLR 638).

5 Neither can they be used to prevent molestation of the other parent or to ban them from living with a particular individual (*D v N (contact order: conditions)* [1997] 2 FLR 797 and *Re D (Residence: Imposition of conditions)* [1996] 2 FLR 281).

7.1.5 Duration of orders

1. Orders end when a child is 16 unless the circumstances are exceptional.

2. No order can be made for a child who has reached 16 unless the circumstances are exceptional.

3. Upon implementation of the A&CA 2002 the court, when making a residence order in favour of a non-parent, can make the order until the child is 18. If that is done there can also be a direction that leave is required to apply to vary or discharge the order.

7.2 APPLYING FOR A SECTION 8 ORDER

7.2.1 Who can apply?

Able to apply for all s8 orders as of right	Able to apply for residence/ contact as of right; leave needed for others	Need leave for all applications
1. Any parent. 2. Any guardian. 3. Anyone with a residence order. 4. Any step-parent / civil partner of a natural parent who has PR. 5. Any special guardian.	1. Step-parent or ex-step parent in relation to whom the child is a child of the family. 2. Person with whom child has lived for three years. 3. If child in care, anyone who has the consent of local authority. 4. If there is a residence order, anyone who has the consent of each person who holds the order. 5. Anyone with the consent of everyone with parental responsibility for the child.	Anyone who is not in the other two columns.

1. If the applicant for leave is not the child who is to be the subject of the order, s10(9) requires the court to consider all the circumstances, in particular:
   - the nature of the proposed application;
   - the applicant's connection with the child;
   - any risk of the application harming the child by disrupting his life;
   - if the child is looked after by a local authority:
     (i) the authorities' plans for the child;
     (ii) the wishes and feelings of the child's parents.
2. If the applicant is the child concerned, the test is whether the child has sufficient understanding to make the application (s10(8)).

7.2.2 Restrictions on applications

1. Anyone who was a foster carer for the child within the last six months may not apply for leave unless:
   - he has the consent of the local authority;
   - he is a relative;
   - the child has lived with him for three years in the last five years (that period decreases to the last year upon implementation of the A&CA 2002).
2. No s8 order, except a residence order, may be made while the child is subject to a care order.
3. Specific issue and prohibited steps cannot be used to achieve a result that could be achieved by a residence or contact order.
4. If a special guardianship order is in place then anyone who would not normally need leave to apply for an order will need leave.

7.2.3 Other considerations

1. Applicants for leave have rights under Article 6 and often Article 8 of the ECHR 1950.
2. The minimum essential protection of these rights was that judges were careful not to dismiss the applications without full inquiry (*Re J (leave to issue application for residence order)* [2003] 1 FLR 114).

7.3 SECTION 91(14) ORDERS

7.3.1 Definition

1. S91(14) gives the court power to prevent anyone named in the order from making an application in relation to a named child without leave of the court.
2. The type of order and length of prohibition should be named in the order.

7.3.2 Usage

1. The order is usually used for vexatious litigants to prevent unreasonable and repeated applications.
2. Orders can, however, be made pre-emptively in cases where the conduct of the applicant is not yet oppressive, or where there was no criticism of the applicant's conduct but the order meets the best interest of the child (*Re M (Care Orders: restricting applications)* [1999] 3 FCR 40).
3. In such cases there needs to be:
   - a particular need for the child to settle;
   - a serious risk that without an order the child or his carers would be placed under unacceptable strain;
   - the degree of restriction imposed must be proportionate to the degree of harm (*Re P (minor) (Residence Order: Child's Welfare)* [1999] 2 FCR 289).
4. If an order is made and leave is sought the applicant must show there is a 'need for renewed judicial investigation' (*Re A (Application for Leave)* [1999] 1 FCR 126, [1998] 1 FLR).
5. The only conditions that can be placed in them is the nature of the application and the duration, which can be without limit of time (*Re S (Children): RE E (A child) (2006)* [2006] EWCA Civ 1190 CA).

7.4 CHILDREN AND DOMESTIC VIOLENCE

1. The existence of domestic violence does not mean that there is automatically no contact with the perpetrator. It is a question of the child's welfare (*Re H (Contact: Domestic Violence)* [July 1998] Fam Law 392).
2. The landmark case of *Re L, Re V, Re M and Re H (Contact: Domestic Violence)* [2000] 3 FLR 334 sets out how allegations of domestic violence should be dealt with.

Allegations of domestic violence, which might affect the outcome of a contact case, should be subject to a finding of fact exercise and be found proven or not proven.

If domestic violence is proven, the court should consider:
- the past and present conduct of the parties towards each other and towards the children;
- the effect on the children and on the residential parent;
- the motivation of the parent seeking contact.

Family judges and magistrates needed to have a heightened awareness of the existence of exposure of children to domestic violence between their parents, and the effect this has on the children.

Re L, Re V, Re M, Re H [2000] 3 FLR 334, Guidelines for domestic violence cases

The court must try to ensure that any risk of harm to the child is minimised and that the safety of the residential parent and child is ensured. Practical arrangements must safeguard them from further harm.

There is no presumption that on proof of domestic violence the violent parent must surmount a *prima facie* barrier to contact.

The ability of the offending parent to recognise their past conduct, to be aware of the need to change and to make genuine efforts to do so is likely to be an important consideration.

3. The court can consider the emotional happiness and stability of the home as well as the need for contact with the absent parent (*M v A (Contact: domestic violence)* [2002] 2 FLR 92).

4. It is important to protect the mental and physical health of the child's carer where they are in real fear for themselves or the children's safety (*Re: H (Contact order) (No 2)* [2002] 1 FLR 22).

5. The court must balance the risk with the child's need to see their parent as in *Re A (Contact: Witness Protection Scheme)* [2005] EWHC 2189 (Fam) where a child in a witness protection scheme had contact via time-delayed video link.

7.5 FAMILY ASSISTANCE ORDERS

1. An order makes available a probation officer, or officer of the local authority, to advise, assist and (where appropriate) befriend:
   - any parent or guardian of the child;
   - any person with whom the child is living or in whose favour a contact order is in force with respect to the child;
   - the child himself.
2. The circumstances must be exceptional.
3. The order requires the consent of every person to be named in the order, other than the child.
4. A direction may require anyone named to allow visits from the family assistance officer and to keep them informed of their address.
5. The order lasts a maximum of six months.
6. If implemented the Children and Adoption Act 2004 will amend these provisons to remove the requirement for exceptional circumstances and to extend the maximum periods to 12 months.

7.6 PROCEDURE FOR SECTION 8 ORDERS

1. An application is made on Form C1.
2. At least 14 days notice must be given to the respondent of the first direction hearing. He must then file a Form C7 acknowledgement within 14 days of service.
3. In exceptional circumstances, applications can be made without notice to the respondent, or the court may abridge the usual time for service.

4. As there is no standard protocol at present for private child law cases, each court has discretion over what direction to give, but they will commonly include the filing of statements and the involvement of the CAFCASS service in filing a s7 report.
5. The matter may require further direction hearings or may be listed immediately for final hearing.

7.7 REPRESENTATION OF CHILDREN IN PRIVATE LAW PROCEEDINGS

7.7.1 Children bringing their own applications for s8 orders

1. A child who is 'the child concerned' may apply under s10(1)(a)(ii) for leave to apply for a Children Act 1989, s8 order. In order to be 'the child concerned' the proposed order must be about the child making the application and not, say, a sibling of the child.
2. The court must be satisfied that the applicant child has sufficient understanding to make the application. This is a similar test to 'Gillick competency' for consent to medical treatment.
3. Leave will not be granted to a child whose interests coincide with those of a parent (or other person) who is already a party to the proceedings (*Re H (Residence Order: Child's application for leave)* [2000] 1 FLR 780).
4. The court should consider whether there was a reasonable prospect of the application succeeding (*Re SC (a minor) (leave to seek residence order)* [1994] 1 FLR 96).
5. A disadvantage of separate representation is that the child will be exposed to hearsay evidence of the parents which it might be better for the child not to hear. A child will only be permitted to bring an application over matters of

importance, not trivial ones (*Re C (residence: child's application for leave)* [1996] 1 FCR 461, [1995] 1 FLR 927).

6. The application should be brought in the High Court. If commenced elsewhere, it must be transferred to the High Court (*Re AD (a minor) (child's wishes)* [1993] 1 FCR 573; *Practice Direction* [1993] 1 All ER 820, [1993] 1 FCR 584).

7. If the child is not the 'child concerned' in the application, e.g. a child is seeking a contact order in relation to a sibling, the test will not be sufficient understanding but the same test as an adult seeking leave (*Re S (a minor) (adopted child: contact)* [1999] 1 All ER 648, [1999] 1 FCR 169, [1998] 2 FLR 897).

8. The general rule is that a child may only bring family proceedings by his 'next friend' and defend any family proceedings by his 'guardian *ad litem*' (Family Proceedings Rules 1991, r 9.2).

9. A child can act without a next friend or guardian where:
   - he has obtained leave of the court; or
   - where a solicitor considers that the child is able, having regard to his understanding, to give instructions in relation to the proceedings and has accepted instructions from the child to act for him (FPR Rule 1991, r 9.2A).

10. A solicitor can assess the understanding of a child but the ultimate decision lies with the court (*Re T (a minor) (Wardship: representation)* [1993] 4 All ER 518).

11. Sufficient understanding includes the child's ability to express their own views, the ability to give evidence, be cross-examined, hear the evidence of the other parties, give instructions and make decisions as matters arise (*Re H (a minor) (role of official solicitor)* [1993] 2 FLR 552).

7.7.2 Children being represented in proceedings brought by adults

1. Children are not automatically parties. They can be made a party and representation may be appointed by the court under FPR Rule r 9.5.

2. This may occur where the interests of the child are separate to the parents to a marked degree, or where they have a particular view point which cannot be represented by the parents (*Re A (a child) (Separate representation in contact proceedings)* [2001] 1 FLR 715; *Re H (Contact Order) (No 2)* [2002] 1 FLR 22).

3. Expert evidence may be called on behalf of a child who is separately represented (*Re H (Contact Order) (No 2)* [2002] 1 FLR 22).

4. The courts have recently commented that the government and the judiciary may have to consider policy issues for the future, such as:
   - whether judges see children to ascertain their wishes and feelings;
   - if that was to become the norm, what training judges should receive;
   - to what extent separate representation should be made available to the child at the heart of the proceedings; and
   - what services should CAFCSS be expected to provide in order to assist the forensic process to ensure that the decision meets Articles 6 and 8 (*Re T (Contact: Alienation: Permission to appeal)* [2003] 1 FLR 531).

5. A guardian for the child can be appointed from CAFCASS, an agency representing children such as National Youth Advocacy Service (NYAS) or, in suitable cases, CAFCASS Legal.

6. CAFCASS Legal will help in the following circumstances (*CAFCASS Practice Notes (Representation of children on*

Family Proceedings Pursuant to FPR 1991 Rule 9.5) [2004] 1 FLR 1188):

- Cases in which the children's division of the OS or CAFCASS Legal previously acted for the child.
- Exceptionally complex international cases where legal or other substantial enquiries abroad will be necessary or there is a dispute as to which country's courts should have jurisdiction over the child's affairs (for example, a case in which two children previously the subject of adoption and then care proceedings in two countries were brought to England and made the subject of further care proceedings here).
- Exceptionally complex adoption proceedings (for example where there is a need to investigate a suspected illegal payment or placement; adoption proceedings following a mistake during fertility treatment involving the use of unauthorised sperm and the circumstances arising in *Flintshire County Council v K* [2001] 2 FLR 476).
- All medical treatment cases where the child is old enough to have views which need to be taken into account or where there are particularly difficult ethical issues such as the withdrawal of treatment, unless the issue arises in existing proceedings already being handled locally when the preferred arrangement will usually be for the matter to be continued to be dealt with locally but with additional advice given by CAFCASS Legal.
- Any freestanding Human Rights applications pursuant to s7(1)(a) HRA 1998 in which it is thought possible and appropriate for any role to be taken by CAFCASS and its officers.
- Other family proceedings in which the welfare of the children is or may be in question may be referred to CAFCASS Legal where they are exceptionally difficult, unusual or sensitive.

- Any additional categories that may be added to this list from time to time.

7.8 ENFORCEMENT OF CONTACT PROCEEDINGS

1. Both European case law and domestic case law emphasise that there is a positive duty on the courts to ensure that contact takes place between parents and children (e.g. *Hansen v Turkey* [2004] 1 FLR 142; *Zwadaka v Poland* [2005] 2 FLR 897; *Re S (Contact: Promoting Relationship with absent parent)* May [2004] Fam Law 387, [2004] 1 FLR 1279; *Re D (Intractable Contact Dispute: Publicity)* [2004] 1 FLR 1226).

2. Existing methods of enforcement may include:
   - Committal to prison (e.g. *M v M (Breaches of Orders: Committal)* [2005] EWCA Civ 1722 [2006] FLR (forthcoming).
   - Use of a s37 direction to request intervention of social services (only available where the threshold criteria in s31 CA 1989 are passed) (e.g. *Re F (Family Proceedings: Section 37 Investigation)* [2005] EWHC 2935 (Fam).
   - Costs order where enforcement is necessary because of breach of an order *(Re T (Order for costs)* [2005] EWCA Civ 311).
   - Transfer to the High Court (e.g. *Re M (Intractable Contact Dispute: Court's Positive Duty)* [2005] EWCA Civ 1090.
   - Transfer of residence order.

3. When implemented the Children and Adoption Act 2004 Part 1 will create new remedies to be inserted into the Children Act 1989:
   - Contact activity directions on an interim order ('a direction requiring an individual who is a party to the proceedings to take part in an activity that promotes contact with the child concerned'), s11A CA 1989.

- Contact activity condition on a final order, s11C CA 1989.
- S11G/H – orders can be monitored for success after the final hearing by a CAFCASS officer/Welsh Family Proceedings Officer.
- Enforcement orders, s11I CA 1989 – between 40 and 200 hours of unpaid work requirements. A warning notice must be inserted in the court order before an enforcement order can be made. They must be necessary to secure compliance and proportionate to the breach.
- Payment for the payment of compensation money, s11O CA 1989. Applies where an individual has, without reasonable cause, failed to comply with a contact order and a relevant person has suffered financial loss by reason of the breach.

CHAPTER 8

SERVICES FOR CHILDREN IN NEED

8.1 LOCAL AUTHORITY'S DUTIES TO INVESTIGATE

8.1.1 Section 47 Children Act 1989

1. Each local authority has a duty to investigate and 'make inquiries' in relation to children within its area where:
   - it is informed that a child who lives or is found within its area is subject to an emergency protection order or is in police protection;
   - it has reasonable cause to suspect that a child who lives or is found within its area is suffering, or likely to suffer significant harm.
2. The local authority must make such inquiries as it considers necessary to enable it to decide whether it should take any action to safeguard or promote the child's welfare.

8.1.2 Section 37 Children Act 1989

1. In private law family proceedings the court may make a s37 direction if:
   - a question of the child's welfare arises;
   - the court thinks a care order or supervision order may be appropriate;
   - the court wishes the local authority to investigate the child's circumstances.
2. A s37 direction requires the local authority to consider whether it should:
   - apply for a care or supervision order;
   - provide services or assistance;
   - take any other action.

3. After the investigation it must report to the court, explaining its decision and reasons.
4. The local authority must take reasonable steps to gain access to the child to carry out their inquiries unless satisfied that they already have adequate information.
5. If denied access, the local authority must apply for an emergency protection order, a child assessment order, a care order or a supervision order – unless satisfied that the child's welfare can be satisfactorily safeguarded without doing so.
6. A s37 direction may be suitable where contact is being denied by one parent without good reason (*M (Intractable Contact Dispute) (Interim Care order)* [2003] 2 FLR 636).

8.2 LOCAL AUTHORITY'S DUTIES TO CHILDREN IN NEED

8.2.1 The general duties of a local authority to children in need

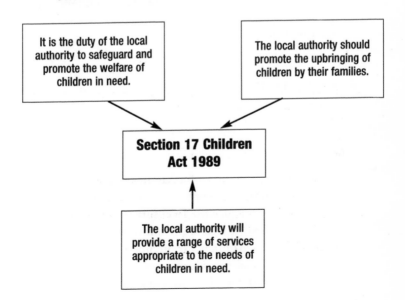

1. A child is in need if:
   - without services being provided, he is unlikely to achieve or maintain a reasonable standard of health or development;
   - without services, his health or development is likely to be seriously impaired;
   - he is disabled.

2. Development includes physical, intellectual, emotional, social or behavioural development. Health is physical or mental.

3. Local authorities must take reasonable steps to identify children in need. The assessment must be a three-stage one of identifying the child's needs, producing a plan and identifying the required services (*R v Tower Hamlets London Borough Council ex p Bradford* [1998] 1 FCR 629).

4. The Lanning inquiry into the death of Victoria Climbié confirmed that that assessment must be of the child's own needs, not just those of her adult carers or whole family.

5. Assistance can include providing accommodation and can be assistance in kind or, in exceptional circumstances, cash. The general s17 duty gives the local authority power to assist with accommodation where other housing law does not help (*R on the application of W v Lambeth Borough Council* [2002] 2 FLR 327).

6. Local authorities must facilitate the provision of services by others, e.g. voluntary organisations, and may delegate their duties.

Schedule 2 Duties of local authority

Para 1(2)	To publish information about services provided by the authority and other organisations. To ensure those who might benefit receive the information.
Para 2	To maintain a register of disabled children.
Para 4	To take reasonable steps to prevent a child suffering ill-treatment or neglect.

Para 6	To provide services designed to minimise the effect on children of their disabilities, and to give them the opportunity to lead as normal a life as possible.
Para 7	To take reasonable steps to reduce the need to bring applications for care or supervision orders.
Para 7	To take reasonable steps to reduce the need to bring criminal proceedings against children and to encourage children not to commit criminal offences.
Para 8	To provide advice, guidance and counselling as appropriate.
Para 8	To provide appropriate occupational, social or cultural activities.
Para 8	To provide appropriate home help.
Para 8	To provide appropriate assistance with travel to take up other services.
Para 8	To provide assistance with a holiday as appropriate.
Para 9	To provide family centres.
Para 10	To take such steps as are reasonably practical to enable a child to live with his family or to promote contact with his family.
Para 11	To have regard to different racial groups when providing day care or encouraging people to be foster parents.

7. It is the child's needs and not the adult's that must be assessed (*R v Tower Hamlets London Borough Council ex p Bradford* [1998] 1 FCR 629 and The Lanning Inquiry).

8. The duties are general and cannot be enforced by any one child (*A v Lambeth London Borough Council* [2002] 2 FCR 289).

8.2.2 Duty to provide day care (s19)

1. Each local authority shall provide day care for children in need under the age of five and not yet at school, as they deem appropriate.
2. For children in need at school, the authority must provide care or supervised activities as appropriate out of school hours and during holidays.
3. It is up to the local authority, not parents, to decide what is an appropriate offer of day care for each child (*R v Barnett LBC ex p B and others* [1993]).
4. A review of day care provisions must be held every three years.

8.2.3 Duty to provide accommodation (s20)

1. The local authority must provide accommodation for children in need if they need it because:
   - no one has parental responsibility for them;
   - they are lost or abandoned;
   - their carer has been prevented from providing suitable accommodation or care.
2. The child's wishes must be ascertained and considered when finding a placement.
3. The accommodation cannot be provided if anyone who has parental responsibility for the child, and is willing and able to accommodate him, objects.

8.3 LOCAL AUTHORITY'S DUTIES TO LOOKED-AFTER CHILDREN

1. Looked-after children include children in care and children provided with accommodation on a voluntary basis.
2. The duties of the local authority are:
   - to safeguard and promote the child's welfare;
   - to make use of their own services for those children;

- before taking steps for that child, to find out the wishes and feelings of the child, parents, anyone with parental responsibility or anyone else whose wishes and feelings are relevant;
- to give due consideration to those wishes and feelings, and the child's religion, race, culture and language;
- to provide accommodation and maintenance for the child;
- to try to find suitable accommodation near the child's home and with siblings.

8.4 REVIEWS FOR LOOKED-AFTER CHILDREN

1. Where children are looked after by the local authority, s26 CA 1989 requires regular review of their cases.
2. The Review Regulations 1991 provide for a review once during the first four weeks, once in the next three months, then every six months thereafter.
3. The A&CA 2002 inserts s26(2)(f) to require a care plan for looked-after children who are not subject to a care order.
4. There must now be an independent reviewing officer to:
   - participate in the child's reviews;
   - monitor the local authority;
   - refer the child's case to CAFCASS where appropriate.

CHAPTER 9
EMERGENCY CHILD PROTECTION

9.1 POLICE PROTECTION

1. Police protection does not require a court order but is a power given to the police under s46 CA 1989.
2. A child is taken into police protection when a constable who has reasonable cause to believe that a child would otherwise be likely to suffer significant harm:
   - removes the child to suitable accommodation and keeps him there; or
   - takes reasonable steps to stop a child being removed from any hospital or a place in which he is being accommodated.
3. Having protected the child, the constable must:
   - inform the local authority, within whose area the child was found, of the steps that have been taken or will be taken for the child, and why;
   - tell the local authority, within whose area the child is ordinarily resident, where the child is being accommodated;
   - inform the child (if he appears capable of understanding):
     (i) what the police have done for him and why;
     (ii) the further steps that may be taken for him;
   - take such steps as are reasonably practicable to discover the wishes and feelings of the child;
   - ensure that the case is looked at by a 'designated officer' (Inspector level);
   - where the child was taken into police protection by being removed to accommodation which is not provided by a local authority or a refuge, he must make sure the child is moved to such accommodation.

4. The following people must be informed about the child's whereabouts, the steps taken or to be taken by the police and their reasons for taking those steps:
   - the child's parents;
   - every person who is not a parent of his but who has parental responsibility for him;
   - any other person with whom the child was living immediately before being taken into police protection.

5. No child can be kept in police protection for more than 72 hours.

6. The child must be released if there is no ongoing reason to believe that the child would be likely to suffer significant harm if released.

7. The police may apply for an Emergency Protection Order for the child.

8. The police do not obtain parental responsibility for the child, but may do what is reasonable in all the circumstances of the case for the purpose of safeguarding or promoting the child's welfare (having regard in particular to the length of the period during which the child will be so protected).

9. The following people are to be allowed such contact as the police think reasonable and in the welfare of the child:
   - the child's parents;
   - any person who is not a parent of the child but who has parental responsibility for him;
   - any person with whom the child was living immediately before he was taken into police protection;
   - any person in whose favour a contact order is in force with respect to the child;
   - any person who is allowed to have contact with the child by virtue of an order under s34; and
   - any person acting on behalf of any of those persons.

9.2 CHILD ASSESSMENT ORDERS

1. Applications for Child Assessment orders may be made by the local authority or the NSPCC.
2. The court must be satisfied that:
   - the applicant has reasonable grounds to suspect the child is suffering or is likely to suffer significant harm;
   - an assessment of the child's health or development is needed to determine whether their beliefs are correct.
3. Child assessment applications are interchangeable with applications for emergency protection orders (EPOs) in the sense that on an application for one the court can make the other.
4. An EPO must be made instead if there are grounds for one and the court thinks it is the more appropriate order.
5. An order lasts seven days from a date specified in the order.
6. The order requires the production of the child to a person named in the order and compliance with any directions in the order. It authorises assessment of the child.
7. A child of sufficient understanding may refuse to submit to the assessment.
8. The assessment may be carried out away from the child's home. If the child is kept away from home the order will specify the contact the child should have with other persons while away.
9. The people entitled to notice of the application are:
   - the child's parents;
   - any person with parental responsibility for the child;
   - a person caring for the child;
   - anyone with a s8 or s34 contact order for the child;
   - the child.

9.3 EMERGENCY PROTECTION ORDERS

Any applicant
There is reasonable cause to believe that the child is likely to suffer significant harm if he is not removed to accommodation provided by or on behalf of the applicant, or if he does not remain in the place in which he is then being accommodated.

Local authority as applicant
- enquiries are being made under section 47(1)(b); and
- those enquiries are being frustrated by access to the child being unreasonably refused; and
- the authority has reasonable cause to believe that access is required urgently.

Grounds for applying for an EPO

Authorised person (NSPCC) as applicant
- There is reasonable cause to suspect that a child is suffering, or is likely to suffer, significant harm.
- The NSPCC is making enquiries with respect to the child's welfare.
- The enquiries are being frustrated by access to the child being unreasonably refused.
- The NSPCC has reasonable cause to believe that access to the child is required as a matter of urgency.

1. EPOs require proof of a likelihood of future harm.
2. The grounds are based on the existence of reasonable cause to 'believe'. This is a low test, not requiring the proof of facts on a balance of probabilities (*R on the application of S v Swindon Borough Council and Another* [2001] FCR 702).
3. The welfare checklist does not apply.
4. An EPO gives the local authority limited parental responsibility for the child concerned. S44(5) provides that they can only take such steps as are resonably required to

safeguard or promote the welfare of the child having regard
to the duration of the order.

5. It authorises:
   - the removal of the child;
   - the keeping of the child in local authority
     accommodation;
   - the prevention of the child being removed from a
     hospital.

6. The order requires any person who has the child to
   produce the child to someone implementing the order.
   The order also makes it a criminal offence to prevent the
   removal of a child in accordance with the order.

7. The order may include a direction for a medical
   examination of the child or an order for contact between
   the child and any other person.

8. Even while the order continues, there is a duty to return
   the child if it seems safe to do so. The child must be
   returned to:
   - the carer from whom the child was removed;
   - a parent;
   - anyone with parental responsibility;
   - with leave of the court to an appropriate person.

9. The child must be allowed to have reasonable contact with:
   - his parents;
   - anyone who has parental responsibility for him;
   - anyone with whom he was living when the order was
     made.

10. Orders last for eight days maximum, with one extension
    only for up to seven days.

11. Applications can be made without notice to the parents,
    who must be told within 48 hours of the order.

12. Applications to discharge cannot be made until 72 hours
    after the order is made.

13. Recent cases have set out principles limiting the use of
    EPOs in the light of human rights concerns:

(a) *X Council v B (Emergency Protection Orders)* [2004] EWCA 2015 [2005] 1 FLR 341

- EPOs are 'terrible and drastic', 'draconian' and 'extremely harsh'.
- The least interventionalist order should be sought.
- It is 'simply unacceptable' for EPOs to be automatically and unthinkingly made for the full eight days. It shouldn't be for any longer than is absolutely necessary to protect the child.
- There is a duty to consider return of the child and thus a duty to keep the case under review day by day.
- There is a duty to give 'reasonable contact'.

(b) *Langley v Liverpool City Council* [2005] EWCA Civ 1173

- Once there is an EPO the police powers under s46 can only be used if it is impracticable to execute an EPO.

(c) *Re X: Emergency Protection Orders* – 17 March [2006] EWHC 510 (Fam)

- EPOs require exceptional justification and extraordinarily compelling reasons. Imminent danger must be actually established.
- Cases of emotional abuse will rarely, if ever, warrant an EPO let alone an application without notice. Cases of sexual abuse where the allegations are inchoate and non-specific, and where there is no evidence of the immediate risk of harm to the child, will rarely warrant an EPO.
- Cases of fabricated or induced illness where there is no medical evidence of immediate risk of direct physical harm to the child will rarely warrant an EPO.
- The evidence in support of an application for an EPO must be full, detailed, precise and compelling.

14. S44A CA 1989 allows an exclusion order to be attached to EPOs where there is reasonable cause to believe that if a 'relevant person' is excluded from the property the test for the EPO would no longer be satisfied. Such an order can be enforced by power of arrest.

CHAPTER 10
CARE AND SUPERVISION ORDERS

10.1 GENERAL PRINCIPLES OF PUBLIC CHILD LAW

1. There should be multi-agency cooperation before an application is made.
2. A multi-disciplinary, multi-agency case conference should be convened, which should aim to recommend an agreed course of action.
3. It should include parents, the child (if of sufficient age and understanding) and other family members. They should be allowed to participate and should be kept informed.
4. No application should be made without clear evidence that provision of services for the child and his family has failed or would be likely to fail to meet the child's needs adequately, and that there is no suitable person prepared to apply to take over care of the child under a residence order.

10.2 CARE ORDERS

10.2.1 Nature of a care order

1. A care order gives the local authority parental responsibility for the child.
2. Parents retain parental responsibility, but the local authority can determine the extent to which they can use it. Parents retain the ability to do 'what is reasonable in the circumstances for the purpose of safeguarding or promoting the child's welfare'.
3. Parents retain:
   - the right to determine the child's religion;
   - the right to appoint a guardian;

- the right to consent to the making of an adoption order, an order freeing the child for adoption, or an order giving parental responsibility to a person who intends to adopt the child abroad;
- the right to consent to or cause the child's surname to be altered.

4. The application should be made by the local authority within whose area the child normally resides or, where the child does not ordinarily reside in the area of a local authority, the authority within whose area any circumstances arose in consequence of which the order is being made.

5. Normal residence is where the child was living immediately before being placed in care. If a child spends time being accommodated in another authority, that time is ignored (*Re BC (a minor) (Care Order: Appropriate Local Authority)* [1995] 3 FCR 598).

6. For 'ordinary residence', any time when the child lives in a school or other institution, or under a supervision order, or while he is being provided with accommodation by or on behalf of a local authority, will be disregarded (*Gateshead Metropolitan Borough Council v L and Another* [1996] 2 FLR 179).

7. Care orders cannot coexist with a residence or supervision order. Parental responsibility orders can run alongside care orders.

8. On an application for a care order, the court may make a supervision order instead.

10.2.2 Parties to the application

1. Everyone with parental responsibility is a party to the application.

2. Other family members need to seek leave to be joined in as parties. This includes fathers without parental responsibility. As a general rule, human rights considerations require that such fathers should be given

leave unless there is a justifiable reason not to (*Re P (Care Proceedings: Father's Application to be Joined as Party)* [2001] FLR 781).

10.2.3 The threshold criteria

1. To make a care order, the court must be satisfied that:
   - the child concerned is suffering, or is likely to suffer, significant harm; and
   - the harm, or likelihood of harm, is attributable to:
     (i) the care given to the child, or likely to be given to him if the order were not made, not being what it would be reasonable to expect a parent to give to him; or
     (ii) the child's being beyond parental control.
2. These threshold criteria must be passed for each child who is the subject of the application.
3. They must be satisfied at the time the order is made, or at the time the child protection process is first put into place if the protection is continuous (*Southwark London Borough Council v B* [1998] 2 FLR 1095).

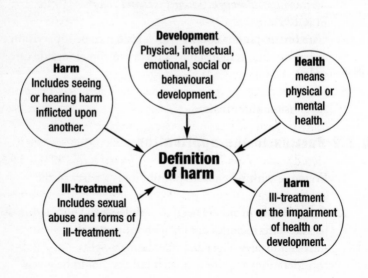

4. The harm must be significant. This means considerable, noteworthy or important (*Humberside County Council v B* [1993] 1 FLR 257).

5. The harm must be proved on the balance of probabilities (*Re H (minors) (Sexual Abuse: Standards of Proof)* (1996) 1 All ER 6).

6. The orders sought must be proportionate to the type and level of harm in a case. The local authority must work with the family and support them unless the risk of harm is so high that the child's welfare requires alternative care (*Re C and B (Care Order: Future Harm)* [2001] 1 FLR 611).

7. The standard of care given is an objective test of the reasonable parent. It is not necessary to show that it must have been the actual parents that harmed the child (*Lancashire County Council v B* [2000] 1 FLR 583).

8. If a court cannot tell which of two parents harmed a child, the child must be treated as if he were at risk from both of them (*Re CB and JB (minors) (Care proceedings: case conduct)* [1998] 2 FCR 313 and *Re O and N* [2003] 1 FLR 1169).

9. Where the parents agree the threshold criteria, the local authority can seek to go back and add to the criteria later if it affects the care of the child (*Re B (Agreed Findings of Fact)* [1998] 2 FLR 968).

10.2.4 The welfare test

1. Even if the threshold criteria are passed, the care order can only be made if it is in the child's welfare.

2. The court must consider the complete range of orders it could make (*Humberside County Council v B* [1993] 1 FCR 613).

3. At the welfare stage, the court cannot take into account any risk of harm in the future if the facts upon which that risk is said to have been based have not been proved at the threshold stage. The court must be satisfied, on the balance

of probabilities, that a future risk exists, and cannot act on mere suspicions (*Re M and R (minors) (sexual abuse: expert evidence)* [1996] 4 All ER 239).

4. In cases where the parent of a child is himself a child, it is the welfare of the child who is the subject of the application which is paramount (*F v Leeds City Council* [1994] 2 FCR 428).

5. Compliance with Article 8 of the ECHR 1950 requires that the order interferes with the family life only in so far as is necessary for the child's welfare.

   - Removal of a child from a delivery room where the mother was not, at the time, showing signs of her mental illness was 'arbitrary and unjustified' (*K & T v Finland* [2000] 2 FLR 79).

   - It is acceptable to deny a father the ability to be involved in proceedings for his child where he had delayed, and to join him in at a very late stage would now breach the child's rights to a fair trial (*Re P: Care Proceedings: Father's application to be joined as party*) [2001] 1 FLR 781).

   - If there is conflict between the rights of an adult and those of a child, the child's prevail (*Yousef v Netherlands* [2003] 1 FLR 210).

   - Article 8 rights include the right to be involved with the procedural aspects of decision making for a child (*Venema v The Netherlands* [2003] 1 FLR 552).

   - However, mere procedural breaches do not necessarily lead to a breach if the parent or child is not adversely affected (*C v Bury MBC* [2002] 2 FLR 868).

10.2.5 The care plan

1. In each case, a local authority must provide a care plan setting out the child's social history and their plans for the child's future. This must be done taking into account the wishes and feelings of the family and the child (*Re R (minors) (care proceedings: care plan)* [1994] 2 FCR 136).

2. The care plan should be 'sufficiently firm and particularised for all concerned to have a reasonably clear picture of the likely way ahead for the child for the foreseeable future'. If there are uncertainties as to the plan, the court may make interim care orders until there is certainty (*Re S (children: care plan)* and *Re W (children: care plan)* [2002] 1 FCR 577).

3. The A&CA 2002 inserts s31A into the CA 1989, making the care plan a statutory requirement in applications where a care order might be made. There is a duty to keep it under review.

4. S31(3A) prohibits the court from making a final care order until it has considered a care plan.

5. The Adoption and Children Act 2006 created amendments to s26 CA 1989 and a new s31A with obligations to keep care plans under review and to appoint a reviewing officer.

10.2.6 The use of interim care orders

1. S38 CA 1989 allows the court to make an interim care order where an application for care or supervision is adjourned or there is a s37 direction. The court must be satisfied that there are reasonable grounds for believing that the threshold criteria are satisfied.

2. Once a care order is made, the local authority has responsibility for the child and the court has no monitoring role. Nor does the guardian who represented the child have any further role in that child's life (*Re T (a minor) (Care order: Conditions)* [1994] 2 FLR 423).

3. Early court decisions held that once the court was sure that a care order was the only option, a final order must be made even if the judge was not happy about the care plan and felt unable to do what was best for the child (*Re S and D (Children: Power of Court)* [1995] 2 FLR 456).

4. The Court of Appeal subsequently suggested a concept of starred care plans, whereby important steps to be taken in

the child's life would be marked in the care plan. In the event that they did not take place, the matter would be returned to court (*Re W and B; Re W (Care Plan)* [2001] 2 FLR 582).

5. The House of Lords disapproved of this idea as being an 'amendment not interpretation' of the CA 1989, and said it was not supported by the HRA 1998.

6. However, it was held that interim care orders may be used even where the court is not going to return the child to the family, if there are uncertainties as to the child's future which ought to be worked out before the court relinquishes its control (*Re S (minors) (Care order: Implementation of care plan); Re W (minors) (Care order: Adequacy of care plan)* [2002] UKHL 10, [2002] 2 WLR 720, [2002] All ER 192, [2002] 1 FLR 815).

7. Interim orders are appropriate where 'the care plan seems inchoate or the passage of a relatively brief period seems bound to see the fulfilment of some event or process vital to planning and deciding the future'.

10.2.7 Statutory review system

1. S26 CA 1989 and the Review of Children's Cases Regulations 1991 require local authorities to review the cases of children whom they are looking after to ensure the care plan still promotes and safeguards the child's welfare.

2. The first review is after four weeks of the child being looked after, then three months, then every six months.

3. The review must include consultation with the child, his parents, anyone with parental responsibility for the child and anyone else whom the local authority thinks is relevant.

10.3 SUPERVISION ORDERS

1. A supervision order puts the child under the supervision of a designated local authority.

2. The threshold criteria must be satisfied before an order can be made.

3. A supervision order does not give a local authority parental responsibility.

4. On an application for a supervision order, the court may make a care order instead.

5. The order may place certain types of requirements on a child.

To comply with any directions which the supervisor may give in the future to:
- live at a certain place;
- present himself to a specified person at a stated time and place;
- participate in activities.

To submit to a medical or psychiatric examination. The order must specify the place and doctor concerned. If the child is old enough to have 'sufficient understanding' they must consent to the examination.

Possible requirements on a supervision order

To keep the supervisor informed of his address and allow home visits.

6. The order can impose conditions on a 'responsible person' to ensure that the child complies with any requirements of directions. A responsible person is anyone with parental responsibility for the child and anyone with whom the child is living. They must consent to the order.

7. An order may last for one year, with possible extension to a maximum of three years. It can only require compliance with direction for requirements for a maximum of 90 days.

8. The orders require supply of services by the authority and cooperation from parents. If these are forthcoming, supervision may be preferred to care as the least interventionist approach (*Re O (a child) (supervision order: future harm)* [2001] 1 FCR 289).

10.4 CONTACT TO A CHILD IN CARE (S34 CA 1989)

1. The local authority has a duty to allow a child in care reasonable contact with:
   - his parents;
   - any guardian;
   - anyone who had a residence order before the care order;
   - anyone with care and control under wardship before the care order.

2. Contact with these people must always be considered before a care order is made.

3. It is for the local authority in the first instance to decide what is reasonable having regard to the welfare of the child. The term 'reasonable' should be determined objectively (*Re P (minors) (contact with children in care)* [1993] 2 FLR 156).

4. If there is a dispute over what is reasonable, or contact is sought by a person not on the above list, the court may order how much contact there should be.

5. Conditions may be placed on the contact order.

6. An order under s34(4) authorises the local authority to refuse contact to people otherwise entitled to it. This is a permissive order allowing an authority to stop contact at once or at a later date.

7. S34(4) orders should not be made pre-emptively as a precautionary measure, but only when a need to stop contact has been shown.

8. The local authority can refuse contact without a court order for up to seven days if it is a matter of urgency and the child's welfare requires it.

9. There is a more general duty for all looked-after children to promote contact with parents, relatives and friends. Such people who are not on the above list may seek leave to apply for an order for contact to a child in care.

10.5 CHALLENGING A LOCAL AUTHORITY DECISION

10.5.1 The complaints system

1. Under s26 CA 1989 each local authority must establish a complaints procedure. It can be used by:
   - any child being looked after by the authority or a child in need;
   - a parent of such a child;
   - anyone with parental responsibility for such a child;
   - a local authority foster parent;
   - anyone else with sufficient interest in the child's welfare.

2. The complaints system only relates to the local authority's duties under Part III of the Children Act 1989.

10.5.2 Judicial review

1. Judicial review may be available to challenge a decision of a local authority in relation to child protection.

2. To succeed, an applicant must show that:
   - the local authority has made a decision that is capable of being reviewed;
   - there is no alternative remedy that has not yet been exhausted;
   - their decision was 'Wednesbury unreasonable', i.e. it was a decision so unreasonable that no reasonable authority could have come to it, or there is a breach of the rules of natural justice;

- the court reviewing the decision should use its discretion to alter the decision (*Re v Lancashire County Council ex p M* [1991] and *R v Kingston Upon Thames Royal Borough Council ex p T* [1994]).

3. However, not all decisions will be amenable to judicial review. The general duties of the local authority to children in need gives them a lot of discretion to use their judgement and expertise. It is for the local authority, not a court, to decide what services should be given to an individual child (*R v Barnett LBC ex p B and others* [1993]).

4. Even when an assessment is done, the general duty does not crystallise so as to be specific to a child and thus enforceable (*A v Lambeth London Borough Council* [2002] 2 FCR 289).

5. Leave to seek judicial review is required from the QBD.

10.5.3 Using the Human Rights Act 1998

1. Human rights issues can be raised within public child law proceedings to influence the outcome. Where possible, these issues should be raised within other family proceedings.

2. However, the higher courts acknowledge that there may be occasions when a decision is made about a child by a local authority which is an interference with the child's or the parent's human rights, but there is no way of using the CA 1989 to put that matter before the courts (*Re S (minors) (Care order: Implementation of care plan); Re W (minors) (Care order: Adequacy of care plan)* [2002] UKHL 10, 2 WLR 720, [2002] All ER 192, [2002] 1 FLR 815).

3. Ss7 and 8 of the HRA 1998 allow freestanding actions for breaches (or proposed breaches) of an individual's human rights by a public authority. Damages and other remedies, such as injunctions, can be awarded.

4. The test under s7 HRA 1998 is different from judicial review. The concept of proportionality requires the reviewing court to assess the balance which the decision maker has struck, not merely whether it is within the range of reasonable decisions (*R (Daly) v Secretary of State for the Home Department* [2001] 2 AC 532).

10.6 NEGLIGENCE BY THE LOCAL AUTHORITY

1. The local authority cannot be held liable for negligence for failing to undertake child protection enquiries or doing so incompetently (*X v Bedfordshire CC and Others* [1995] 2 AC 633, [1995] 2 FLR 276).
2. A claim for negligence can be brought where the use of discretion results in a duty of care for a child arising. A care order imposes such a duty (*Barrett v Enfield London Borough Council* [1999] 2 FLR 426).
3. Where a local authority, contrary to foster carer's requests, placed a child known to be sexually abusive with a family, resulting in other children being abused, the children could sue for assault and the parents for consequent distress (*W and others v Essex County Council and another* [2000] 1 FLR 657).
4. The authority were liable both in negligence and negligent misstatement for false assurances to the family.
5. A claim for negligence for damages flowing from an unsuitable placement of a child may cease at the point when the risk is knowingly accepted by the carers (*AA and B v Essex County Council* [2003] 1 FLR 615).
6. A failure to plan properly for children in care is a breach of statutory duty (*F v Lambeth London Borough Council* [2002] 1 FLR 217).

10.7 THE PROCEDURE IN PUBLIC LAW CASES

10.7.1 Principles behind the procedure

1. The procedure in public child law cases is now governed by the *Practice Direction (Care Cases: Judicial Continuity and Judicial Case Management)* [2003] 2 FLR 719, which introduces the protocol for Judicial Case Management in Public Law Children Act cases.
2. The purpose of the scheme is to ensure that:
   - cases are dealt with in accordance with the overriding objective;
   - that there are no unacceptable delays in the hearing and determination of cases;
   - that (unless there are exceptional or unforeseen circumstances) every care case is finally determined within 40 weeks of the application being issued.
3. The overriding objective of the scheme is to ensure that the court can deal with every care case:
   - justly, expeditiously and with the minimum of delay;
   - in ways which ensure, so far as is practicable, that:
     (i) the parties are on an equal footing;
     (ii) the welfare of the children is safeguarded;
     (iii) distress to all parties is minimised;
   - in ways which are proportionate to the gravity and complexity of the issues, and the nature and extent of the intervention proposed in the private and family life of the children and adults involved.
4. The practice direction stresses the need to avoid undue delay and the fact that European cases on Article 6 require 'exceptional diligence' (*Johansen v Norway* [1996] 23 EHRR 33).
5. The key principles of the scheme are:
   - judicial continuity – each case is to be managed by not more than two judges;

- active case management by the judiciary;
- consistency by standardisation of steps and the use of standard procedures and orders;
- the case management conference where the issues will be identified and the timetables fixed.
6. Each court will have a plan of how the protocol will be implemented locally.
7. The protocol includes the following standard documents:
   - a standard direction form;
   - a case management questionnaire, which deals with issues of complexity/urgency/evidence needed, timetables and directions sought;
   - a case management checklist comprising 63 questions to prompt advocates to ensure the case is prepared thoroughly;
   - a witness non-availability template;
   - a PRH checklist comprising 22 questions.

10.7.2 The protocol regime

1. On the day of issue:
   - The applicant local authority must file a Form C1, and a Form C13 setting out all its reasons for applying for a care order and attaching any necessary schedules with the facts and matters relied on.
   - The court will fix a hearing date not later than day six.
   - The court will appoint a guardian for the child and ask CAFCASS to identify a guardian.
2. By day three:
   - CAFCASS must respond to the request for a guardian.
   - The guardian, if appointed at once, must appoint a solicitor for the child. If there is to be a delay in appointment the court will decide whether to appoint a solicitor.
   - The local authority must file and serve all parties with the application, any court orders, an initial social work

statement and chronology, the core or initial assessment reports, any s37 report and any other evidence.

3. By day six:
   - The first hearing in the FPC will take place, which will consider inter alia that there has been proper service, who should be parties, the hearing of contested interim orders and whether there should be a transfer to the County Court.
   - If the matter is not to be transferred, the FPC will hold a case management hearing at which they will timetable further steps and give case management directions.

4. By day 11, if the matter is transferred to the care centre:
   - Two judges will be allocated the case, and the file prepared with standard documents to aid case management.
   - There will be an allocation hearing, which will consider inter alia transfer to the High Court, timetabling and the case management checklist, and give directions as to the filing of statements and evidence.

5. The next step will be a Case Management Conference (CMC), which will be held between days 15 and 60, depending on the evidence which needs to be gathered.
   - Not later than five days before the CMC the local authority prepares a completed case management questionnaire and all their 'case management documents'.
   - Two days before the CMC, the parties file a position statement, a completed case management questionnaire and any other documents the court orders.
   - Before the CMC, there is an advocates' meeting to discuss the issues, the case management questionnaires and checklists, and whether experts are needed. A composite schedule of issues must be drafted.
   - The court must be given details of the availability of all witnesses and advocates.

- At the CMC, all case management issues will be considered, a final hearing and pre-hearing review listed, and further direction given to ensure the case remains on track and that all expert and social work assessments will be ready for the hearing.

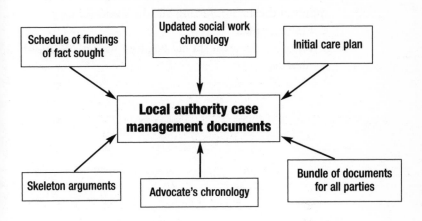

6. If the case requires it, there may then be a further directions hearing if there is a change of circumstances or significant non-compliance with the direction given by the court.

7. Otherwise, the next stage is the Pre-Hearing Review (PHR), which should take place by week 37.
   - In the week before there will be an advocates' meeting to identify and narrow the issues, consider the PHR checklist and compile a composite schedule of issues.
   - Ideally, the judge who will do the final hearing should also do the PHR.
   - The court will consider the checklist and the schedule of issues, confirm hearing dates and give any directions needed to update the case management documents and bundle.
   - If all parties confirm the case is ready and all agree, the PHR may be dispensed with or dealt with on paper or by electronic means.

8. The final hearing should take place by week 40.

- Two days before the final hearing, the parties will file the case management documents required by the court at the PHR and prepare a court bundle.

- At the hearing, a judgement must be given setting out the reason for the decision, and annexing the agreed or approved documents setting out the threshold criteria and the care plan.

- A reserved judgement should be given within 20 days of the hearing.

CHAPTER 11

ADOPTION: THE ADOPTION AND CHILDREN ACT 2002

11.1 THE CORE PRINCIPLES

1. An adoption agency and the court must now make the child's welfare the paramount consideration, a test which is in line with the CA 1989 (s1(2)).
2. However, this principle goes further than the CA 1989 as, for adoption decisions, the child's welfare throughout his life is relevant, not just during his or her minority. Part of considering if adoption is in the child's welfare will be considering whether other orders such as residence or special guardianship are better alternatives.
3. The court and adoption agency must at all times bear in mind that, in general, any delay in coming to a decision is likely to prejudice the child's welfare (s1(3)).
4. The agency and court must consider the range of orders available under the CA 1989, and this Act and the court must not make an order unless doing so is better for the child than not making an order at all.
5. An agency must give due consideration to the child's religious persuasion, racial origin and cultural and linguistic background.

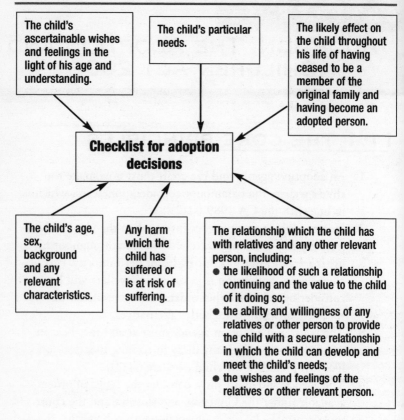

The child's ascertainable wishes and feelings in the light of his age and understanding.

The child's particular needs.

The likely effect on the child throughout his life of having ceased to be a member of the original family and having become an adopted person.

Checklist for adoption decisions

The child's age, sex, background and any relevant characteristics.

Any harm which the child has suffered or is at risk of suffering.

The relationship which the child has with relatives and any other relevant person, including:
● the likelihood of such a relationship continuing and the value to the child of it doing so;
● the ability and willingness of any relatives or other person to provide the child with a secure relationship in which the child can develop and meet the child's needs;
● the wishes and feelings of the relatives or other relevant person.

11.2 WHO MAY APPLY AND WHO MAY BE ADOPTED?

1. Applications to adopt can be made by:
   ● a single person;
   ● a married couple;
   ● a couple 'living in an enduring family relationship' of the same or a different sex;
   ● a step-parent or the partner of the child's parent if they are in an enduring family relationship.

2. A single adopter must be over 21. For a couple, both must be over 21 save where a natural parent is one of the adopters. Then the natural parent must be over 18 and their partner over 21.

3. Where a couple adopts, at least one must be domiciled in the British Isles, and both must have been habitually resident in the British Isles for at least one year before the application.

4. The Act requires regulations to ensure that agencies give proper regard to the need for stability and permanence in the relationship of a couple when assessing them as suitable to adopt.

5. It is possible to make an order for a child who is over 18 as long as the application was made before they achieved that age. The order must be made before they are 19.

11.3 PRELIMINARY REQUIREMENTS

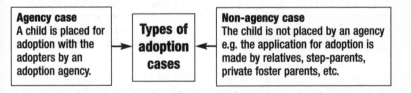

Agency case
A child is placed for adoption with the adopters by an adoption agency.

Types of adoption cases

Non-agency case
The child is not placed by an agency e.g. the application for adoption is made by relatives, step-parents, private foster parents, etc.

1. In an agency case, the child must have had his or her home with the applicants for ten weeks before the application

2. In a non-agency case, the child must have had his or her home with the applicant for:
   - six months if the applicant is a step-parent or partner of a natural parent;
   - one year if the applicants are local authority foster parents for the child;
   - a cumulative period of three years within the last five years for other applicants.

3. Where the conditions are not satisfied, an application can still be made with leave of the court.

4. In an agency case, the agency must submit a report to the court on the suitability of the applicants and any issues arising from the checklist.

5. In a non-agency case, the proposed adopters must give the local authority notice of their application to adopt not more than two years and not less than three months before making the application. The local authority must then investigate the suitability of the applicants and submit a report.

6. If leave to apply is needed, the leave must be obtained before the notice to the local authority is given.

7. Before an adoption order can be made, the court must be satisfied that the agency or local authority has had sufficient opportunities to see the child with the adopters in 'the home environment'.

11.4 THE PRE-CONDITIONS FOR PLACING A CHILD FOR ADOPTION

1. A child cannot be placed for adoption unless it is at least six weeks old.

2. Parents may give their consent to a child being placed for adoption. Such consent must be 'given unconditionally and with full understanding of what is involved' (s52(5)).

3. Once consent is given, it can be withdrawn up to the issuing of an adoption application, although this does not result in the immediate return of the child until the local authority's application for a placement order is determined or they agree to return the child.

4. The consent may be to placement with particular adopters or with any prospective adopters whom the local authority may choose. Consent to the subsequent adoption may be given at the same time.

5. If there is no parental consent, the child cannot be placed until the local authority has obtained a placement order under s21.

11.5 PLACEMENT ORDERS

1. Freeing orders have been replaced by placement orders, which must be obtained before the child is placed with prospective adopters. This will make it easier for parents to contest the plan for adoption before the child becomes used to a new home and carers.
2. The order authorises a local authority to place a child for adoption with any prospective adopters chosen by them.
3. The placement may then last until:
   - it is revoked by the court;
   - an adoption order is made;
   - the child reaches 18.
4. Any person may seek revocation, but a parent who applies for the revocation of a placement order must obtain leave and to do so must show that there has been a change in circumstances since the placement order was made (s24).
5. For a placement order to be made, the court must be satisfied that:
   - the child is already subject to a care order; or
   - the 'threshold criteria' for a care order under s31 CA 1989 are established; or
   - the child has no parent or guardian.
6. The court must also be satisfied that:
   - there is unequivocal parental consent to the placement of the child with any adopters that might be chosen by the local authority; or
   - that parental consent should be dispensed with.
7. It is mandatory for the local authority to apply for a placement order where:
   - the child is placed for adoption or accommodated under s20 CA 1989;

- no adoption agency has authority by way of parental consent to place the child for adoption;
- the child has no parent or guardian or the local authority considers that the 'threshold criteria' are met and is satisfied that the child ought to be placed for adoption.

8. A placement order gives the adoption agency parental responsibility. When placement is actually made with a family the prospective adopters also obtain it. The local authority may determine the extent to which natural parents and proposed adopters may exercise their parental responsibility.

9. The placement order ends any previous orders for contact under s8 or s34 CA 1989, and new applications must be made under s26 while the child is subject to the placement order.

10. It is clear that contact with the birth family and/or friends of the child may continue after adoption, as the A&CA 2002 provides that an application under s8 CA 1989 can be made and heard at the same time as the adoption order.

11.6 ADOPTION ORDERS

1. An adoption order ends all parental responsibility previously held, except that which the adopters acquired under a placement order.

2. An adoption by a spouse/civil partner or partner of a natural parent of a child will not extinguish the parental responsibility held by that parent, so the natural parent is no longer forced to adopt their own child with the spouse/civil partner or partner.

3. Before an order is made, the court must consider whether there should be arrangements allowing any person contact with the child after adoption.

The court is satisfied, in the case of each parent or guardian, that: ● he or she consents to the making of the adoption order; or ● he or she has given advance consent to the order and has not withdrawn it and agrees to the adoption; or ● his or her consent should be dispensed with.	The child has been placed for adoption with parental consent and: ● the consent of the mother was given when the child was at least six weeks old; or ● the child was placed for adoption under a placement order; and ● no parent or guardian opposes the making of an adoption order.

One of three conditions must be satisfied before an adoption order can be made

The child is free for adoption.

11.7 DISPENSING WITH PARENTAL CONSENT

There are now only two possible grounds for dispensing with parental consent to a placement order or an adoption order:
● the court is satisfied that the parent or guardian cannot be found or is incapable of giving consent; or
● the welfare of the child requires the dispensation of consent.

11.8 INFORMATION ABOUT ADOPTION

11.8.1 The Adoption and Children Act Register

1. The Register began in August 2001 and contains details of children waiting to be adopted and approved adoptive

families, with a view to speeding up the linking of children with new families

2. It is not open to the public and is used by agencies seeking to place a child with as little delay as possible.

11.8.2 The Adoption Contact Register

1. The A&CA 2002 places a duty on the Registrar General to compile an adoption contact register.
2. It is in two parts:
   - Part 1 – information about adopted persons;
   - Part 2 – information about relatives of adopted persons. 'Relatives' is defined as relatives by blood, half-blood or marriage other than relatives by adoption.
3. The register is not open to public inspection, but on the application of the adopted person information will be given to them about any relative who has registered as wishing to have contact with them. The registered relatives have no right to request information about their adopted relative.
4. The register is open to children adopted from overseas and their relatives.

11.8.3 Information about adopted persons

1. The A&CA 2002 gives the adopted person access to all information held by the agency necessary for him to apply for a copy of his original birth certificate.
2. The High Court may prevent that information being given in exceptional circumstances.
3. The Act contains mechanisms for the obtaining of some other information about an adopted person's background from the adoption agency, but the agency is given an element of discretion as to what may be disclosed.

CHAPTER 12

FINANCES BEFORE A DIVORCE

12.1 MAINTENANCE AGREEMENTS

1. Spouses may agree a level of maintenance to be paid by one to the other upon their separation.
2. To be valid the agreement must either be in a formal deed or conform with the general laws of contract, including the need for good consideration for the maintenance.
3. Maintenance agreements remain valid after divorce unless overridden by a court order (*Adams v Adams* [1941] 1 KB 536, [1941] 1 All ER 334).
4. Agreements include separation deeds which do not otherwise contain provision as to financial arrangements.
5. The agreement cannot oust the jurisdiction of the court to make such future orders (*Hyman v Hyman* [1929] AC 601).
6. The High Court, County Court and Magistrates' Court have jurisdiction to alter maintenance agreements.
7. The grounds on which they may do so are:
   - a change in the circumstances (including a change foreseen by the parties when they made the agreement) which means that the agreement should be altered so as to make different financial arrangements; or
   - the agreement does not contain proper financial arrangements with respect to any child of the family.
8. The court may vary or revoke any financial arrangements contained in the agreement, or insert into it financial arrangements for the benefit of one of the spouses or a child of the family.
9. These powers in relation to a child can now only be exercised where the Child Support Agency does not have jurisdiction.

10. Magistrates' Courts may only deal with unsecured periodic payments.

11. The applicable test is whether the new arrangement appears to the court to be just, having regard to all the circumstances, including, if relevant, the matters considered by the court when making orders for children of the family on divorce.

12. A written maintenance agreement for a child will give the courts jurisdiction to make a consent order even where the CSA has jurisdiction.

13. However, the terms of a maintenance agreement cannot be effective to prevent one partner making an application to the CSA (s9(4) Child Support Act 1991).

12.2 APPLICATIONS UNDER s27 MATRIMONIAL CAUSES ACT 1973

1. One of the parties must:
   - be domiciled in England and Wales; or
   - be resident in England and Wales; or
   - have been habitually resident in England and Wales for a year before the application.

2. The grounds for a s27 order are that the other party has failed to provide reasonable maintenance for the applicant; or (subject to the CSA having jurisdiction) has failed to provide, or to make a proper contribution towards, reasonable maintenance for any child of the family.

3. The factors to be considered are the same as for financial relief after a divorce. The question will be whether the money actually being paid is in the same region as an order which would have been made if the parties had divorced or judicially separated.

4. The orders are the same as those available on a divorce, save that there is no power to make a property adjustment order.

5. A divorce subsequent to a s27 order does not automatically revoke the order, but re-marriage of a recipient spouse/civil partner would revoke a periodic payment order.
6. Interim orders can be made until the court has the information needed to make a final decision.

12.3 APPLICATIONS IN THE MAGISTRATES' COURT UNDER THE DOMESTIC PROCEEDINGS AND MAGISTRATES' COURT ACT 1978

1. Either spouse may apply for an order under s2 on the grounds that the other:
   - has failed to provide reasonable maintenance for the applicant; or
   - has failed to provide, or to make a proper contribution towards, reasonable maintenance for any child of the family;
   - has behaved in such a way that the applicant cannot reasonably be expected to live with the respondent; or
   - has deserted the applicant.
2. The orders that can be made are:
   - periodical payments for such term as may be specified;
   - a lump sum not exceeding £1000. This may be deferred or be paid by instalments;
   - subject to the CSA, periodical payments for the benefit of a child of the family and for such term as may be specified;
   - a lump sum direct to or for the benefit of the child of the family not exceeding £1000 for each child.
3. Periodical payment orders for children can only be made where the CSA does not have jurisdiction.
4. The first consideration is the welfare of the child. The factors to be taken into account mirror the s25 MCA 1973 criteria for ancillary relief after a divorce.

5. A consent order under s6 Domestic Proceedings and Magistrates' Court Act 1978 (DPMCA 1978) may be made by the court simply on the grounds that the parties have agreed to the financial provision in it and the arrangements are not contrary to justice. In such cases there is no £1000 limit on any agreed lump sum.

6. An application for an order under s7 DPMCA 1978 may be made where the parties have lived apart for more than three months (not including desertion cases) and one has made periodic payments to the other for three months.

7. A s7 order may only order periodic payments at a rate no higher than the aggregate of the payments actually made in the last three months.

8. If the court thinks its powers under s7 are insufficient it can treat the application as one under s2 because its view means that the respondent must not be providing reasonable maintenance.

9. Interim maintenance orders can be made on any application under the DPMCA 1978. Interim orders expire on the first to occur of:

   ● any date in the order;
   ● three months from the making of the order;
   ● the making of a final order.

   An interim order can be renewed to extend the period of validity.

10. On applications for a variation of periodic payments the court can vary or revoke and may impose a second lump sum up to £1000.

11. Orders under ss2 or 6 can be made even if the parties are living together. However, if they continue to live together, or reconcile and then cohabit for six moths, any final order ceases to have effect, save for any order made for a child.

12. Orders under s7 cease to have effect when the parties resume living together (s 25).

CHAPTER 13

ANCILLARY RELIEF – FINANCES AFTER A DIVORCE/DISSOLUTION OF CIVIL PARTNERSHIP

13.1 THE ORDERS AVAILABLE FOR ADULTS

13.1.1 The difference between spouses/civil partners

1. The remedies for spouses are those in the Matrimonial Causes Act 1973. Since same sex couples cannot enter into a marriage these remedies are unavailable to them but are in effect replicated in Sched 5 Civil Partnership Act 2004. The table indicates the equivalent section numbers. It is anticipated that the case law will be applied to both types of relationship. In order to keep the information concise the notes below refer only to the MCA 1973 section numbers. Reference to the table should be made for those dealing with civil partnerships.

Provisions in MCA 1973	Equivalent in Sch 5 CPA 2004
s21(a) Periodical payments during marriage	Part 9 para 41(a)
s21(b) Secured periodical payments during marriage	Part 9 para 41(b)
s21(c) Lump sum during marriage	Part 9 para 41(c)
s21A Pension sharing order definition	Part 4 para 16
s22 Maintenance pending suit	Part 8
s23 (a) Periodic payments	Part 1 para 2(1)(a)
s23(b) Secured periodic payments	Part 1 para 2(1)(b)
s23(c) Lump sum(s)	Part 1 para 2(1)(c)
s23(d) Periodic payments to/for a child	Part 1 para 2(1)(d)
s23(f) Lump sum to/for a child	Part 1 para 2(1)(e)
s24 Property adjustment order	Part 2
s24A Sale of property	Part 3
s24B-D Pension sharing	Part 4
s25 Criteria to take into consideration	Part 5
s25A Clean breaks	Part 5 para 23
s25B Pension criteria	Part 6 para 24/25
s25C Pension lump sums	Part 6 para 26
	Part 7 pension fund compensation to be in matters which the court are to take into account
s37 Avoidance of disposition	Part 14
Variations	Part 11

Periodical payments

1. S23(1) provides for periodical payments orders for spouses ('spousal maintenance').
2. An order may be for a nominal sum only (e.g. 5p per annum) to keep the claim open in case of a future change of circumstances.
3. Factors justifying a nominal sum include:
   - continuing responsibility to raise and provide a home for a young child;

- the unlikelihood of the recipient being able to earn an income to support herself in the foreseeable future;
- the length of the marriage; and
- a wife's entitlement to choose between working, and home-making and child rearing when still married without being forced to or being afraid of what might happen if the marriage broke down (*SRJ v DWJ* [1999] 3 FCR 153).

4. An order for decree nisi is needed before a final order for periodical payments can be effective.

5. Orders may contain provisions building in automatic increases in the future, e.g. by the same percentage each year as the husband's pay increase or the rate of inflation. This prevents the need for variation applications based solely on the effect of inflation reducing the spending power of the recipient (*Sharp v Sharp* [1984] FLR 752).

6. A 'Connell' order makes a final order for periodic payments to the wife to include a sum for the children to be reduced pound for pound by any child benefit received. This bridges any gap between the final ancillary relief hearing and a forthcoming calculation by the CSA (*Dorney-Kingdon v Dorney-Kingdon* [2000] 3 FCR 20).

7. The same method can be used to deal with other uncertain forms of future income, such as tax credits.

8. A periodical payments order may be open ended ('until further order'), or specify a term during which the payments are to be made. The order can be backdated, but only as far back as the date the application was made.

9. A direction can be made under s28(1A) preventing an application to extend a limited term.

10. If a term maintenance order is made without such a direction any application to extend the time limit must be made while the order is still current (*G v G (Periodic payments: jurisdiction)* [1997] 1 FLR).

11. Maintenance ceases automatically on the death or the remarriage of the recipient. Cohabitation does not

automatically end maintenance, but most orders are drafted to provide that it should do so.

12. Periodical payments may be 'secured' on a capital asset of the payer. That asset remains the property of the payer but is subject to a charge to enable enforcement or, in the alternative, is used as a source from which the periodical payments are taken.

13. Periodical payments may be varied, suspended temporarily, revived or dismissed.

13.1.2 Lump sum orders

1. A decree nisi or decree of judicial separation or nullity is needed before a lump sum order can be made.

2. The lump sum can be deferred to a later date or made payable in instalments, which can be secured.

3. The order can include provisions for interest to be due until the lump sum is paid.

4. Except for clean breaks after a variation application, only one lump sum order can be made.

5. It can be for expenses incurred by the recipient in maintaining herself before the application was made.

6. A lump sum order can be made for a spouse who has remarried as long as the application was made before the wedding.

7. Lump sum orders are often linked to property adjustment orders or orders for sale, with the events all taking place at the same time.

8. If there will be capital available in the foreseeable future a lump sum application may be adjourned if it is just, such as when an inheritance is likely within a short period of time or an unquantifiable bonus will be received (*MT v MT (financial provision: lump sum)* [1992] 1 FLR 362 and *D v D (Lump Sum order: Adjournment of Application)* April [2001] Fam Law 254).

9. Orders can be made where there is no cash available but the potential payer has a borrowing capacity or a capital asset that can be realised.

10. A lump sum can only be varied if it is to be made in instalments or is a pension attachment. The time for payment may be extended (*Masefield v Alexander (lump sum: extension of time)* [1995] 1 FLR 100).

13.1.3 Property adjustment orders

1. Property adjustment orders are not effective until decree absolute, and their substantive terms cannot be varied (*Omelian v Omelian* [1996] 2 FLR 306).

2. Property includes:
   - land;
   - personal property;
   - money;
   - shares;
   - policies;
   - house contents;
   - contingent assets;
   - choses in action;
   - weekly private tenancies and council tenancies;
   - property owned absolutely or to which the spouse is entitled to in reversion.

Outright transfer from one party to another of all or part of a property
- Often done as part of a clean break.
- If the legal title is to be transferred and not just the equitable interest, the recipient spouse will need either to secure the release of the other from any mortgage or to indemnify him for the payments.

Transfer with charge back
- Suitable where fairness requires one spouse to continue to occupy the property but it is unfair that the other loses all their capital interest.
- The charge may be for a fixed sum (the disadvantage of this is that the sum may be eroded by rising house costs) or as a percentage of the equity.
- The order will contain 'trigger events' when the charge becomes payable (*Belcher v Belcher* [1995] 2 FCR 143).
- Often used as an alternative to a trust for sale as they are nearer to a clean break.

Transfer with lump sum
- In effect one party buys the other out of his interest in the property by paying a lump sum in exchange for a transfer of property to them.

Varieties of property adjustment orders

Creation of trusts for sale
- The house is vested in both parties' joint names on a trust for sale, or the existing trust is varied. In each case the new shares are specified by the court.
- The order will contain a 'triggering event' at which point a delayed order for sale is activated. The trust is flexible, so the trigger may be anything the court or the parties decide. Common forms of this trust are:
    (i) **a Mesher order** – the trigger being the children reaching 18 or the end of full-time education, whichever is later (*Mesher v Mesher and Hall* (1973) [1980] 1 All ER 126);
    (ii) **a Martin order** – the trigger is the wife's remarriage or cohabitation or death, whichever is first (*Martin v Martin* [1977] 3 All ER 762).
- Orders must consider all future eventualities, such as who is to be responsible for future repairs or improvements to the property, or whether the remaining spouse should be allowed to move and transfer the charge to a new property.
- Disadvantages of continued trusts include the fact they are anti-clean break, and the difficulties of predicting housing needs in the future.
- They may now gather increased popularity as a way of achieving a fair settlement that avoids discrimination by 'lending' one spouse's capital to the other for only so long as she has responsibility for the children (*Elliot v Elliot* [2001] 1 FCR 477).
- However, they may be inappropriate where the spouse staying in the home is to give an ongoing contribution to the family by raising the children, and where the end result would be a significant disadvantage to the wife in terms of her capital position at the trigger event but only a modest advantage to the husband (*B v B (Mesher Order)* [2003] 2 FLR 285).

13.1.4 Orders for sale

- A court may require the sale of any property in which the parties have a beneficial interest.
- The power can only be exercised if the court is also making an order for a secured periodical payments order, a lump sum or a property adjustment order.

- The order does not take effect until decree absolute is granted.
- The order may deal with consequential issues, such as the payment of bills until sale or the conveyancing arrangements.

13.1.5 Pension orders

1. Traditionally, pensions were often ignored as they were not assets which were going to be available to the parties in the foreseeable future.
2. However, this caused injustice as they could be the major asset of the family and non-working spouses were discriminated against.
3. The only remedy at first was to 'offset' the pension – compensate for its loss by allocation of more capital to the spouse without the pension, if such capital was available.
4. Even since the introduction of special pension orders their use is permitted rather than required of the court, as there is no 'system of entitlement-driven pension-loss compensation' (*T v T (Financial relief: pensions)* [1998] 1 FLR 1073).
5. Courts have commented on the difficulties of valuing pensions and of predicting the suitability of a pension order being made well before the fund becomes payable (*Burrow v Burrow Feb* [1999] 1 FLR 508 Fam Law).
6. Care should be taken not to treat a future contingent income fund as being the same as capital which is available at the time of the divorce, even though the parties are obliged to value a fund by the cash equivalent transfer value (*Maskell v Maskell* [2003] 1 FLR 1138).
7. Earmarking (now called attachment) was a compromise remedy while the implications for tax and pension law of pension sharing were resolved.
   - Orders deal with the benefits payable from the fund on retirement.

- The court can attach part of the lump sum, income or the death-in-service benefit of a pension.
- A widows's benefit cannot be attached and is always lost to the divorcing spouse, making it available for a new spouse.
- The attached benefits are payable directly from the fund to the recipient on the scheme member's retirement.
- The order must be expressed in percentage terms.
- It can set an age at which the scheme member must take their benefits.
- It can specify the proportion of income that must be commuted to a lump sum.
- Attachment orders are a type of lump sum or periodical payments order and the same rules apply, e.g. on remarriage (*T v T (Financial relief: pensions)* [1998] 1 FLR 1073).
- Other disadvantages of attachment are that the benefits cannot be taken at a different time from the spouse, that no extra contributions can be made and that no separate death-in-service benefits arise.

8. Pension sharing orders.
   - These orders allow the court to split the pension fund at the time of the divorce with orders transferring 'sharable rights in a pension'.
   - The recipient spouse then acquires a fund in their own name whether by becoming a member of the original scheme or by transferring the sharable rights to another pension provider.
   - The recipient spouse can thus receive her pension at a different time from her spouse and can nominate her own death in service benefits.
   - Pension sharing is not available after a judicial separation.
   - To gain access to the remedy, the petition must have been filed after 1st December 2000.
   - There may only be one pension sharing order per pension per marriage.

- It is possible to share a pension share and a pension which is already in payment.
- It is not a breach of Article 8 human rights if the effect of a pension sharing order is that one spouse is able to receive the money before the other according to the rules of the scheme (*R (Smith) v Secretary of State for Defence and Secretary of State for Work and Pensions* (2005) 1 FLR 97, EWHC 1797 (Admin)).

13.2 ORDERS AVAILABLE FOR CHILDREN

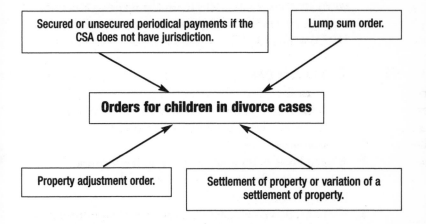

1. Orders are available for 'children of the family' – natural children of both parties and a child who has been treated as a child of the family, other than a foster child.
2. Periodical payments are only available for a child to whom the Child Support legislation does not apply, for example, children in further education, step-children or children whose parents are working overseas and not paid from an office in this country.
3. Top-up orders may also be applied for over and above CSA assessments where the absent parent is a high earner or there is a need to cover the costs of school fees or of a disability.

4. Adult children may receive periodical payments while in education or training for a vocation or profession or if there are 'special circumstances' irrespective of any income they may have of their own.

13.3 THE SECTION 25 CRITERIA

13.3.1. Children's welfare comes first

1. First consideration must be given to the welfare, while still a minor, of any child of the family not yet 18.
2. Courts are not obliged to consider the welfare of the child when an adult. Thus, they are usually denied a share of capital into adulthood (*Chaimberlain v Chaimberlain* [1973] 1 WLR 1557).

13.3.2 Clean breaks

1. Where the court is considering orders in relation to an adult, it has a duty to consider whether a clean break would be appropriate.
2. A clean break is an order terminating the financial obligations of the parties towards each other as soon after decree absolute as is possible.
3. Clean breaks can be extended into death by dismissing the parties claims under the Inheritance (Provision for Families and Dependants) Act 1975 if the court considers it just to do so.
4. If an immediate clean break cannot be achieved, the court must consider a deferred clean break.
5. A deferred clean break will require periodical payments only for 'such a term as would, in the opinion of the court, be sufficient to allow the party in whose favour the order is made to adjust without undue hardship to the termination of his or her financial dependence on the other party'. In *McFarlane v McFarlane* [2006] UKHL 24 the House of Lords thought it unfair to impose a term on

maintenance, believing it better to make the husband come back to seek a later clean break when he could afford it. A term maintenance order would have required the wife to show exeptional circumstances as to why it should continue. The Court of Appeal decision that the wife should be required to save up excess income to achieve a clean break was rejected.

6. An order for term maintenance may contain a s28 direction preventing application to extend the length of the term.

7. If there is no such direction the application must be made before the term expires, although the variation may be made after the term ends (*Jones v Jones* [2000] 2 FLR 307).

8. A parent's obligation to maintain a child cannot be capitalised and so cannot be subject to a clean break.

9. The court may impose a clean break on a variation application by dismissing a periodical payments order and making a lump sum, property adjustment or pension order.

13.3.3 Considerations for adults

1. The income, earning capacity, property and other financial resources which each of the parties to the marriage has or is likely to have in the foreseeable future, including, in the case of earning capacity, any increase in that capacity which it would, in the opinion of the court, be reasonable to expect a party to the marriage to take steps to acquire.

   • Earning capacity includes overtime or the ability to retrain to earn better money.

   • Money available from trust funds can be a resource. The test is whether the money is in reality available to the party (*Browne v Browne* [1989] 1 FLR 291, [1989] Fam Law 147, *T v T and others (joiner of third parties)* [1996] 2 FLR 357). In *Beverley Anne Charman v John Robert Charman* [2006] EWCH 1879 (Fam) the husband's argument that a trust fund was for future generations and should not be touched was rejected on the facts.

Detailed questions were allowed of the trust at the preparation stage to allow the court to ascertain how much of a resource it was to the parties.

- Financial support from family or friends can be a resource (*M v M (Maintenance Pending Suit)* July [2002] Fam Law 511, [2002] 2 FR 123).

- Orders cannot be made against third-party benefactors, but an order can indicate 'judicial encouragement' for ongoing provision (*Thomas v Thomas* [1985] 2 FLR 668).

- Earning capacity should not necessarily be assumed, especially where a spouse has been out of the job market for a long period (*Barrett v Barrett* [1988] 2 FLR 516).

- Earning capacity may decrease, e.g. if a company is in genuine downturn, or because of other s25 factors like disability or age (*Scheeres v Scheeres* Jan [1999] 1 FLR 241).

- A new partner's income may be relevant if they are married or cohabiting or intending to do so. There is no one definition of cohabitation but the court will look at the daily life of the parties looking at the nature, stability and permanence of the relationship and the number of shared activities (*Kimber v Kimber* [2000] 1 FLR 383 and *K v K (periodical Payment: Cohabitation* [2005] EWCA 2886 (Fam)).

- The new partner has no duty to maintain their partner's spouse, so their income is only indirectly relevant to the extent that she is a financial support or a burden to the spouse (*Slater v Slater* [1982] 3 FLR).

- A received inheritance is an asset taken into account, but will be regarded as a special contribution to the marriage. It is unlikely to be ring-fenced if needs cannot be met without using it (*White v White* [2000] 2 FLR 981).

- A future inheritance is rarely relevant because it cannot be certain whether a spouse will inherit, when they will do so or what they will receive. It may, however, be possible to adjourn a lump sum application until the inheritance is known (*MT v MT (Financial Provisions: Lump Sums)* [1992] FLR 362).

2. The financial needs, obligations and responsibilities which each of the parties to the marriage has or is likely to have in the foreseeable future.

   - In big money cases a fair settlement may be reached without allowing extra money for a spouse with a new child but in smaller money cases where every penny has to be counted it may not be possible to ignore the legal and moral responsibility of one spouse to maintain a new child (*H-J v H-J (Financial Provision: Equality)* March [2002] Fam Law).

   - Housing is a need, but there is no absolute right to be able to buy a new house; a party may be adequately housed in rented accommodation or with family (*Piglowska v Piglowska* [1999] 2 FLR 763).

   - However, where there are children, if it is possible for both parents to be re-housed this should be a priority to allow staying in contact with the absent parent (*M v B (Ancillary Proceedings: Lump Sum)* [1998] 1 FLR 53).

3. The standard of living enjoyed by the family before the breakdown of the marriage.

   - The standard of living no longer has to be preserved but must be taken into account.

4. The age of each party to the marriage and the duration of the marriage.

   - The duration of a marriage is measured from the wedding date to separation, but the assets are valued at the time of the hearing, taking into account changes since separation (*Kokosinski v Kokosinski* [1980] 1 All ER 1106). However, prior cohabitation leading seamlessly to marriage can increase the length of the marriage (*Co v Co* [2004] 1 FLR 1095).

   - All orders are available after short marriages, but a maintenance order is not 'a meal ticket for life' and is always susceptible to variation (*C v C (Financial Relief: Short Marriage)* [1997] 2 FLR 27).

- In a short marriage the capital acquired during the marriage is available to be shared equally but the length of the marriage may lead the court to treat pre-owned property differently depending on all the circumstances and what is fair (*Foster v Foster* [2003] 1 FLR 299 and *Miller v Miller* [2006] UKHL 24).

5. Any physical or mental disability of either of the parties to the marriage.

6. The contributions which each of the parties has made or is likely in the foreseeable future to make to the welfare of the family, including any contribution by looking after the home or caring for the family.

   - Contributions in kind to the running of the family are to be treated equally to financial contributions (*White v White* [2000] 2 FLR 981).

   - Continuing to care for children after divorce has been said to constitute an ongoing contribution to the marriage by mothers with residence (*B v B (Mesher Order)* [2003] 2 FLR 285; *M v L (Financial Relief After Overseas Divorce* [2003] 2 FLR 425).

   - A gift or financial support from one spouse's parents can be treated as a contribution by that spouse towards joint assets (*White v White* [2000] 2 FLR 981).

   - The fact that a spouse has given up a career to care for the family may, in big money cases, entitle her to 'compensation' for lost earning capacity (*McFarlane v McFarlane* [2006] UKHL 26).

7. The conduct of each of the parties, if that conduct is such that it would, in the opinion of the court, be inequitable to disregard it.

   - The previous test was that the conduct must be 'gross and inequitable'. Unless the conduct passes this current test the reason for the breakdown of the marriage is not relevant (*Miller v Miller* [2006] UKHL 26).

   - Misconduct within the litigation, such as failure to disclose documents or breach of orders, may result in an order for costs.

- Misconduct within the relationship may alter the order made for division of assets (*Young v Young* [1998] 2 FLR 113; *Tavoulareas v Tavoulareas* [1998] 2 FLR 418).
- Conduct that reduces assets or income, or increases the needs of the other party is most relevant (*Martin v Martin* [1976] 3 All ER 625; *B v B (Financial Provision: Welfare of Child and Conduct* March [2002]).
- Where a spouse's litigation misconduct meant that there was an unclear picture as to the extent of his wealth, the court is entitled to draw adverse inferences (*Al-Kahatib v Masry* [2002] 1 FLR 1053).
- Conduct need not be misconduct, but may refer to the way in which the parties have arranged their finances between them during the marriage (*Parra v Parra* [2003] FLR 943).

A failure to make full and frank financial disclosure (*Robinson v Robinson (No 2)* [1985] Fam law 250).

The husband attacked his wife with a razor, causing injuries that made it impossible for her to continue nursing. The settlement reflected the fact that he was the one that should bear the loss of the family income (*Jones v Jones* [1976] Fam 8).

The husband abducted the child of the marriage, causing his own imprisonment. Thus, the mother had increased legal costs and the loss of a child and spousal maintenance. In addition, the husband transferred money to his mother in Italy putting it beyond the jurisdiction of the court (*B v B (Financial Provision: Welfare of Child and Conduct* [March 2002] Fam Law).

Examples of conduct which the courts have found it inequitable to ignore

The husband 'embarked on a subterfuge to strip the equity from the matrimonial home'. He was ordered to bear the main brunt of the fraudulently obtained mortgage (*Le Foe v Le Foe and Woolich* [2001] 2 FLR 970).

The husband indecently assaulted the children and lost his job as a result (*S v S* [1982] Fam Law 183).

The husband frittered away assets by reckless living and speculation (*Martin v Martin* [1976] 3 AU ER 625).

8. In the case of proceedings for divorce or nullity of marriage, the value to each of the parties to the marriage of any benefit (for example, a pension) which, by reason of the dissolution or annulment of the marriage, that party will lose the chance of acquiring.

   - On divorce or annulment a spouse will lose his or her entitlement to a widow(er)'s pension.
   - They also lose the benefit of their spouse's pension which they would have shared in spending had they remained together as a couple.

13.3.4 Considerations for children

1. Where the court is considering making an order for a periodic payment, lump sum, order for sale or property adjustment order in relation to a child, the court must consider:
   - the financial needs of the child;
   - the income, earning capacity (if any), property and other financial resources of a child. Trust money is a resource (*J v J (C intervening)* [1989] 1 All ER 1121);
   - any physical or mental disability of the child;
   - the manner in which the child was being, and in which the parties to the marriage expected him to be, educated or trained;
   - the considerations mentioned in s 25(2)(a), (b), (c) and (e).

2. If the court is considering an application for these orders in relation to a step-parent, the court must consider:
   - whether that party assumed any responsibility for that child's maintenance and, if so, the extent to which and the basis upon which that party assumed responsibility, and the length of time for which that party assumed such responsibility;
   - whether in assuming that responsibility the party did so knowing that the child was not his own;
   - the liability of any other person to maintain the child.

13.4 AGREEMENTS BETWEEN THE SPOUSES

13.4.1 Pre-nuptial agreements

1. Contracts between spouses specifying division of assets on divorce were traditionally void as being against public policy.
2. Practically, courts were also concerned about unfairness to one spouse resulting from the difficulty of predicting in advance what a fair division of assets would be.
3. For a time, they were of 'limited significance', especially where their purpose is to limit the quantum of settlement (*F v F (Ancillary Relief: Substantial Assets)* [1995] 2 FLR 45).
4. More account was given to contracts specifying in which forum marital disputes should be litigated (*S v S (Divorce Staying Proceedings)* [1997] 2 FLR 100).
5. More recently, contracts have been classed as 'conduct', or as 'all the circumstances of the case', and should be taken into account (*M v M (Prenuptial Agreement)* March [2001] Fam Law 177).
6. The courts will put the child's welfare first, then ask if an injustice would occur to either party if the contract were upheld (*K v K (Ancillary Relief: Prenuptial Agreement)* [2003] 1 FLR 120).

13.4.2 Edgar settlements

1. Agreements made after the separation or at the time of the separation can comprise correspondence, a deed or an unsealed consent order.
2. Spouses cannot exclude the court's jurisdiction to deal with ancillary relief applications (*Hyman v Hyman* [1982] AC 601).
3. The general rule is that 'formal agreements, properly and fairly arrived at with competent legal advice, should not be

displaced unless there are good and substantial grounds for concluding that an injustice will be done by holding the parties to the terms of their agreement' (*Edgar v Edgar* (1981) FLR 19).

4. Those grounds may include:
   - undue pressure;
   - exploitation of a dominant position;
   - inadequate knowledge;
   - bad legal advice;
   - an important change of circumstances overlooked or unknown at the time of making the agreement.

5. Ordinary contractual principles do not apply, as the court retains its full discretion over what order to make (*Xydias v Xydias* [1999] 1 FLR).

6. Edgar settlements are also a form of 'conduct'.

7. Important questions for the court to ask are:
   - How did the agreement come to be made?
   - Did the parties themselves attach any importance to it?
   - Have the parties themselves acted upon it?
   - In the light of those answers, should the agreement be persuasive as to the orders to be made? (*G v G (Financial Provision)* [2000] 2 FLR 32.)

8. The fact that one party might have done better by going to court is not a ground to allow them to resile from the agreement.

9. The totality of the circumstances are to be regarded. They include the financial, social, personal, religious and cultural aspects of the agreement (*X v X (Y intervening)* [2002] 1 FLR 508).

13.5 INTERIM ORDERS

13.5.1 Maintenance pending suit

1. The court can make an order for interim periodic payments for the maintenance of one spouse by the other (s22 MCA 1973).

2. Such payments can be term limited, running from a date beginning with the date of divorce petition for as long as the court thinks reasonable.

3. Maintenance pending suit can be ordered from the issue of the divorce until the decree nisi. After that, an interim periodical payments order can be made.

4. A party can apply for interim maintenance or maintenance pending suit at any stage in the proceedings.

5. The court will look at making a temporary order sufficient to meet basic, immediate and temporary needs (*Peacock v Peacock* [1984] 1 All ER 1069).

6. If there appear to be sufficient assets, the usual exercise is to balance needs against resources and thus come to a temporary figure until the whole question of the division of the matrimonial property can be decided (*T v T (Financial Provision)* [1990] FCR 169).

7. The court has a wide discretion and is not bound by the s25 criteria, but will look to create a holding position based on past spending (*F v F (Ancillary Relief: Substantial Assets)* [1995] 2 FLR).

8. Maintenance pending suit can include an element to cover legal fees (*A v A (Maintenance Pending Suit: Provision of Legal Fees)* [2001] 1 FLR 377). That might be appropriate where the client has no capital, cannot raise a litigation loan and cannot persuade her solictors to take a charge over the end results of the litigation (*Moses-Taiga v Taiga* [2005] EWCA Civ 1013).

9. Parties must prove any change of circumstances since the marriage ended (*M v M (Maintenance Pending Suit)* July [2002] Fam Law 511, [2002] 2 FR 123).

13.5.2 Interim lump sums/property adjustment orders

1. *Barry v Barry* [1992] 2 FLR 233 seemed to open the doors for interim lump sum orders by way of direction. This has been overturned (*Wicks v Wicks* [1998] 1 FLR 470).

- The Court of Appeal would have liked to make an interim lump sum order but declined to use inherent jurisdiction in an area so controlled by statute.
- In *Wicks*, the wife owned the house in her sole name so the husband's matrimonial home rights prevented her selling without his consent.
- The Matrimonial Causes Act 1973 makes no provision for interim lump sums.

2. Family Law Act 1996 s15 and Sched 2, para 3 introduces interim lump sums but was never brought into force.
3. Once a party has invoked the Matrimonial Causes Act 1973 the civil law, such as s14 Trustees of Land Act 1996, should not be used to deal with the property, as any order made can then be varied by property adjustment order (*Tee v Tee and Hillman* [1999] 2 FLR 613).

13.5.3 Variation of orders

1. Orders which can be varied are:
   - interim maintenance orders;
   - a periodic payments order;
   - a secured periodic payments order;
   - a lump sum payable by installments;
   - a deferred lump sum order including attached pension lump sums;
   - an order for a settlement of property, or for a variation of settlement after judicial separation where decree is being rescinded, or an application for divorce has been made;
   - an order for sale of a property;
   - a pension-sharing order which is made at a time before the decree has been made absolute.
2. S31 MCA 1973 gives the court power to vary, discharge, suspend temporarily and revive orders.
3. Applications to vary must be made during the lifetime of the order (*T v T (Financial Provision)* [1988] 1 FLR 480).

The actual variation, however, can be ordered after the expiration of the original order (*Jones v Jones* [2001] Fam 96, [2000] 2 FCR 201).

4. The court must look at all the circumstances of the case afresh.

5. There is no statutory requirement that those circumstances must have changed, but in reality it will be rare for an order to be varied otherwise.

6. The Family Law Act 1996 and the Welfare Reform and Pensions Act 1999 inserted provisions for a clean break on an application to vary periodic payments.

7. If the court discharges a periodic payments order, or varies it to impose a term, it may also make a lump sum order, a property adjustment order, a pension-sharing order on a pension which has not been previously shared, and at the same time prevent any further applications for maintenance.

8. For pension-sharing orders the petition must have been before 1st December 2000.

9. The court, when imposing a clean break, must have regard to all the circumstances of the case, including any change in any of the matters to which the court had had regard when making the original order (*Harris v Harris* [2001] 1 FCR 68).

10. Where the payer's fortunes have increased, it is no longer possible to seek a variation of a spousal maintenance order giving the payee more than her budgeted needs. The power of the court to make a lump sum on variation is not to re-open capital claims but to compensate the recipient for her loss of monthly payments (*Pearce v Pearce* [2003] FLR 1144).

13.6 THE GENERAL APPROACHES OF THE COURTS

13.6.1 Historical position

1. In the early 1970s, the guideline was that the wife and children should receive one-third of the assets (*Wachtel v Wachtel* [1973] 1 All ER 829).
2. Subsequently, needs became predominant. A common approach was to assess the applicant's reasonable requirements according to their standard of living, and found an order on that *(Conran v Conran* [1997] 2 FLR 615; *Preston v Preston* [1982] Fam 17 and *Dart v Dart* [1996] 2 FLR 286).
3. Needs became a 'glass ceiling' in high money cases, with wives receiving enough to maintain their lifestyles but a small percentage of the total marital assets.

13.6.2 *White v White*

The progress of *White v White*

First instance
- Assets of £4.6 million (£193,000 in Mrs W's sole name, £2,668,000 in joint names, £1,783,500 in Mr W's sole name).
- Much of that was a farm run under a joint partnership deed giving each 50% on dissolution.
- Mrs W seeks 50% of all marital assets on divorce.
- Holman J awards her £980,000 for her 'reasonable requirements'. Mr W retains the rest.
- Mrs W appeals.

Court of Appeal
- Mrs W appeals and gets £1.5 million for her 'reasonable needs'.
- After costs, this amounts to one-fifth of the total assets.
- Both spouses appeal.

> **House of Lords**
> ● Lord Nicholls maintained the Court of Appeal decision on quantum.
> ● His judgement changes the basis of assessment from needs to finding a fair settelement using the s25 criteria then applying a 'cross check of equality'.
> ● A new chain of cases is started.

1. This was described as a 'big money case' because the parties' means outstripped their needs.
2. Equal division of assets is not the correct starting point for division and there is no presumption that 50-50 division should be the end result.
3. However, equality is a relevant consideration. There can be no discrimination based on the roles of breadwinner and homemaker, which are both contributions to the marriage.
4. After reaching a proposed settlement based on weighing all the s25 criteria, a 'cross check of equality' should be applied to ensure that neither spouse has been discriminated against because of their gender or chosen role in the marriage.
5. It is permissible to depart from equal division, but there must be good reasons, not based on discrimination.
6. The needs of one party cannot be a determinative and limiting factor while the other is left with a much greater share of the marital assets.

13.6.3 Post *White v White* case law

1. Illiquid assets like businesses might have to be sold to achieve fairness, but not if that would cripple the financial position of the family (*N v N (Financial Provision: Sale of Company)* May [2001] Fam Law 347).
2. Early post-*White* cases allowed a special business talent to be an 'exceptional contribution' justifying unequal division (*Cowan v Cowan* [2001] 2 FLR 191).
3. Later cases refuted this, saying it would be 'repugnant if the court had to draw up a merit table in which fine graduations of contribution gave rise to a marginally

increased or decreased share in the family asset' (*H-J v H-J (Financial Provision: Equality)* March [2002] Fam Law 176).

4. Special contribution remains a legitimate possibility but requires exceptional circumstances. A good idea, initiative, entrepreneurial skill, extensive hard work or exceeded expectations are alone insufficient. High earnings alone may not suffice either (*Lambert v Lambert* [2003] 1 FLR 139; *Charman v Charman* [2006] EWCH 1879 (Fam)).

5. Working and lending money to a family company while bringing up the children is 'part and parcel of marriage', not exceptional contribution (*Norris v Norris* [2003] FLR 1142).

6. Spouses should share equally in both 'safe' and 'risky' assets (*Wells v Wells* [2002] 2 FLR 97; *Charman v Charman* [2006] EWCH 1879 (Fam)).

7. Problems with the liquidity of asset can be a reason to depart from equality (*P v P* Sept [2002] Fam Law 657, 2 FLR 1075).

8. Claw-backs or payments by instalments can exceptionally be used to deal with assets expected to fall in after the order (*Parra v Parra* [2003] FLR 943).

9. Equality does not necessarily mean 50-50 division of the assets, rather 'putting the parties in a position of broadly equal financial muscle' (*G v G (Financial Provision: equal Division)* October [2002] Fam Law 792).

10. There is no duty to do a detailed critical appraisal of the performance of each of the parties during the marriage. There should be a broad-brush approach (*Lambert v Lambert* [2003] 1 FLR 139; *Parra v Parra* [2003] FLR 943).

11. All assets existing are considered, but, certainly where assets outstrip needs, pre-marital assets will be separated from 'marital acquest property'. The length of the marriage and needs will be salient factors in deciding how to divide the former.

13.7 THE STATUTORY CHARGE

1. Public funding is available for ancillary relief applications for spouses with limited resources.
2. Solicitors' costs are paid directly by the Legal Services Commisison and must be repaid by the client from any assets put into issue in the proceedings, which are then 'recovered or preserved'.
3. Assets never in dispute between the parties are not subject to this 'statutory charge' in favour of the LSC.
4. Periodic payments, including those attached from a pension, are not subject to the charge.
5. In the event that all the assets recovered or preserved are being used to provide a home for the assisted person and/or their dependents, the loan can be placed as a legal charge on the property (a 'deferred statutory charge'). Interest will accrue but no monthly payments are required.

13.8 THE PROCEDURE

1. Before issue of proceedings, negotiations and enquiries must be conducted in accordance with the pre-action protocol (*Practice Direction* July [2000] Fam Law, [2000] FLR 997).
2. The aims of the pre-action protocol are to ensure that:
   - pre-application discovery and negotiation takes place in appropriate cases;
   - where there is pre-application disclosure it is dealt with cost effectively and in line with the overriding objectives of the Family Proceedings (Amendment Rules) 1999;
   - the parties are in a position to settle the case fairly and early without litigation.
3. Once proceedings are issued, the court can look back to see if the Protocol is complied with and may impose a costs order if it was ignored.

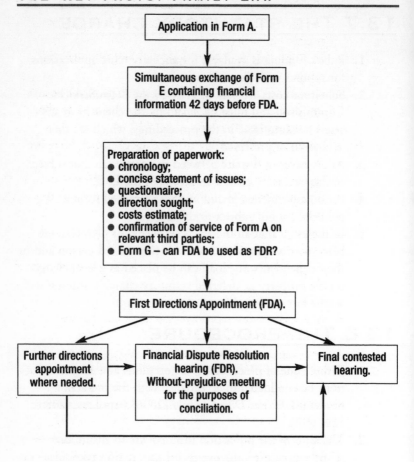

4. The court system is contained in the Family Proceedings (Amendment) Rules 1999, which comprise a new procedural code.
5. The overriding objective of the scheme is to enable cases to be dealt with justly, which means:
   - ensuring that the parties are on an equal footing;
   - saving expense;
   - dealing with the case in ways which are proportionate to the amount of money involved, the importance of the

case, the complexity of the issues and the financial position of each party;

- ensuring that the case is dealt with expeditiously and fairly;
- allotting to the case an appropriate share of the court's resources, while taking into account the need to allot resources to other cases.

6. The judiciary will 'actively manage' cases, which includes:
   - identifying the issues at an early stage;
   - regulating the extent of discovery of documents and expert evidence so that they are proportionate to the issues in question;
   - helping the parties to settle the whole or part of the case;
   - fixing timetables or otherwise controlling the progress of the case;
   - making use of technology;
   - giving directions to ensure that the trial of a case proceeds quickly and efficiently.

7. Application is made in Form A indicating the type of orders sought. The court on issue allocates a first direction appointment (FDA) which must be between 10 and 14 weeks later. The Form is served on the respondent within four days.

8. The application will be in the County Court, unless the divorce is in the High Court or the complexity, difficulty or gravity of the issues involved justify a transfer to the High Court (*Practice Direction (Family Division: Business Distribution)* [1992] 1 WLR 586).

9. A Financial Information Form (Form E) must be exchanged simultaneously with the other party 42 days before the FDA. No other information can be given or requested without the court's permission.

10. At least 14 days before the FDA the parties must file and serve:
    - a questionnaire setting out by reference to the concise statement of issues any further documentation and

information requested from the other party or a
statement that no information and documents are
required;
- a concise statement of issues;
- a chronology;
- a costs estimate;
- confirmation that pension trustees have been served any
application for a pensions order;
- a notice in Form G stating whether that party will be in
a position at the first appointment to proceed on that
occasion to an FDR appointment.

11. At the FDA the district judge will:
- determine the extent to which each questionnaire will
be answered and what documents shall be produced;
- give directions as to the valuation of assets and
instruction of independent experts;
- give directions on any evidence sought to be adduced by
any party and as to any chronologies or schedules to be
filed;
- order a Form P to be completed if there is an
application for pension attachment or sharing further
information about the pension is required.

12. Any information required which is in the possession or
control of a third party may be obtained by using the
inspection appointment procedure, which requires the
applicant to show that the documents are necessary for
disposing fairly of the application and allows the third
party to raise objections.

13. The next step is a Financial Dispute Resolution hearing
(FDR), a without-prejudice hearing held for the purposes
of conciliation, in front of a judge who will have no further
involvement in the case other than to make a consent
order.

14. Not less than seven days before the FDR, the parties must
file all offers and proposals made and at the FDR must
attempt to reach settlement of the dispute by making and
properly considering offers and proposals.

15. Judges may give guidance on what they consider to be a proper settlement, but may only make orders by agreement or to direct matters forward to another FDR or final hearing (*Rose v Rose* [2002] 1 FLR 978).

16. Rule 2.69 provides that either party to the application may, at any time, make a written offer to the other party, 'without prejudice except as to costs' relating to any issue. The court will only see this offer at the FDR or after a final order has been made and costs are to be considered.

17. If an order is made that is more advantageous than an offer made by the other party, the court must, unless it considers it unjust to do so, order that the other party pay any costs incurred after the date beginning 28 days after the offer was made.

18. Not less than 14 days before a final hearing the applicant files an open statement setting out precisely what orders they seek. The respondent files one seven days later.

19. Interim maintenance applications can be made at any time. There must be two weeks between application and hearing. If Form E has not been filed, both parties file a short affidavit setting out the basis of the application.

20. If the parties reach agreement, a consent order may be submitted to the court for approval at any time, accompanied by a Statement of Information form.

13.9 COSTS RULES

1. For cases commenced after April 2006 the general rule is that the court will make no order as to costs.

2. The court may make an order for costs at any stage of the proceedings where it considers it appropriate to so do because of the unreasonable conduct of a party in relation to the proceedings.

3. The court will, when deciding what to do about costs, consider all the circumstances, including:

- the conduct of all the parties whether the proceedings, or any part of them, had to be brought due to the failure of a party to comply with a previous order;
- whether a party has been wholly or substantially unsuccessful in relation to any particular issue in the proceedings;
- an open offer to settle brought to the court's attention;
- conduct would include:
  (i) conduct before as well as during the proceedings;
  (ii) whether it was reasonable for a party to raise, pursue or contest a particular allegation or issue the manner in which the party has pursued or responded to a particular issue.

CHAPTER 14

THE CHILD SUPPORT AGENCY

14.1 JURISDICTION

1. A new system was introduced in 1991 to standardise child support payments and remove the discretionary regime from the courts. A white paper was published on 13 December 2006 to set out proposed changes to create a more streamlined agency but no further details of changes are available at the time of publication.
2. The existing system requires parents on benefits to go through the CSA to obtain child maintenance.
3. Use of the CSA is voluntary for other parents.
4. Parents with care who receive state benefits are obliged to provide information about the absent parent.
5. Failure to do so may result in a reduced benefits direction reducing benefit payments by up to 40% for three years.
6. Reduced benefit directions cannot be made against a carer where there would be 'a risk of her, or any children living with her, suffering harm or undue distress as a result'.
7. Payments will be collected, even if the benefits system recoups the money from the recipient, leaving them no better off.

14.1.1 Which children?

1. One or both parents must be 'non-resident', i.e. the child does not live with them in the same household.
2. The child must live with a 'person with care', i.e. not:
   - a local authority;
   - a person caring for a 'looked-after child' unless they are also that child's parent.

3. The child must not have been married.
4. The child must be:
   - under 16;
   - under 19 and receiving full-time education (which is not advanced education) at a recognised establishment;
   - under 18 and registered for work, or training under work-based training for young people and not engaged in remunerative work.

14.1.2 Which parents?

Both parents and the child must be habitually resident in the UK, except that the non-resident parent may be:
- employed abroad in the Civil Service;
- an armed forces member (including a reservist);
- employed abroad by a company who makes payment details from the UK.

14.1.3 The CSA and court orders

1. No application can be made under the Child Support Act 1991 s4 if there is in force:
   - a written maintenance agreement made before 05/04/93;
   - a maintenance order before 03/03/03;
   - a maintenance order made on or after 03/03/03 and in force for less than one year.
2. If the CSA has jurisdiction, the courts have no powers to order child maintenance except for:
   - cases where the CSA does not have jurisdiction;
   - when the order is for step-children and 'children of the family';
   - children who are 17 or 18 years old and not in education;
   - financially dependent adult children;
   - top-up orders for high earners;
   - orders for additional educational expenses;

- orders for expenses for a disabled or blind child;
- lump sums/property adjustment orders;
- orders against a person with care who is not a parent;
- consent orders where there is a prior written agreement (which may be in the recital to the order) and the order made is for the same amount (Child Maintenance (Written Agreements) Order 1993).
- The court can vary a validly made order.

3. For orders made since 3/3/03 the order only excludes CSA jurisdiction for one year. Variations after 03/03/03 do not restart the one-year period.

4. The court may make a Segal order – an order for spousal periodic payments where credit is required to be given for any sums payable under a CSA calculation (*Dorney-Kingdom v Dorney-Kingdom* [2000] 3 FCR 20).

5. Segal orders require the wife to be entitled to a substantive maintenance order for herself.

6. The parties may agree that in order to give the court jurisdiction, they enter into a written agreement leading to a consent order, then immediately invite the court to vary that order (*V v V (Child Maintenance: Periodical Payments)* [2001] 2 FLR 417).

14.2 CALCULATIONS

14.2.1 Default rate

1. The default rate is payable while the CSA works out the long-term rate payable.

2. It is a set rate based on average payment levels:

Number of relevant children	Payment due per week
1	£30
2	£40
3	£50

3. If there are two or more children and two or more persons with care the sum is apportioned between the children.

14.2.2 Basic rate

1. Applies where net income is over £200 per week. The sum due is a percentage of the non-resident parent's weekly net income:
   - 15% where he has one qualifying child;
   - 20% where he has two qualifying children;
   - 25% where he has three or more qualifying children.
2. Where a paying parent has a child or children at home the same percentage is knocked off the net income as an allowance before the percentages are applied again for the children who do not live with the payer.
3. There is ceiling on net income of £2000 per week, giving a maximum CSA payment of £500 per week.

14.2.3 Reduced rate

1. Applies if neither of the following two options apply and the non-resident parent's net weekly income is between £100 and £200.
2. Takes into account the higher proportion of income taken up on basic living costs for low paid parents.
3. Cannot be less than £5 per week.
4. Formula is in the Child Support (Maintenance Calculations and Special Cases) Regulations 2001 (SI 2001/155), F + (A 5 T) where:
   - F is the flat rate liability applicable to the non-resident parent;
   - A is the amount of the non-resident parent's net weekly income between £100 and £200;
   - T is the percentage determined in accordance with the following table:

	One qualifying child of the non-resident parent				Two qualifying children of the non-resident parent				Three or more qualifying children of the non-resident parent			
Number of relevant other children of the non-resident parent	0	1	2	3 or more	0	1	2	3 or more	0	1	2	3 or more
T (%)	25	20.5	19	17.5	35	29	27	25	45	37.5	35	32.5

14.2.4 Flat rate

1. This is £5 if the nil rate does not apply and the net weekly income is £100 or less or the payer or his partner receives welfare benefits or state pensions or allowances.
2. A lower flat rate of £2.50 is payable if the nil rate does not apply and:
   - the non-resident parent has a partner who is also a non-resident parent;
   - the partner is a person with respect to whom a maintenance calculation is in force; and
   - the partner receives any benefit.

14.2.5 Nil rate

The payer earns less than £5 per week or is:
- a student;
- a child;
- a prisoner;
- a person who is 16 or 17 years old and in receipt of income support or income-based jobseeker's allowance;
- a person receiving an allowance in respect of work-based training for young people or, in Scotland, Skillseekers training;
- a person in a residential care home or nursing home who gets a pension, benefit or allowance and has the

whole or part of the cost of his accommodation met by a local authority;

- a patient in hospital who is in receipt of a benefit which has been reduced for a long stay.

14.2.6 Shared care

1. For basic or reduced rates the reductions where the non-resident parent has care of the child overnight are:
   - 52 to 103 nights reduced by $1/7$;
   - 104 to 155 nights by $2/7$;
   - 156 to 174 by $3/7$;
   - 175 nights or more by 50%, plus a deduction of £7 per child.
2. The sum cannot reduce below £5.
3. If the flat rate is payable because the parent or partner is on benefits, then if there is shared care for at least 52 nights, that sum payable is nil.
4. The child must stay at the same address as the non-resident parent.
5. If the child is in the care of the local authority and basic or reduced rate apply, the sums reduce as per the following table.

Nights in care	Fraction to subtract
52 – 103	$1/7$
104 – 155	$2/7$
156 – 207	$3/7$
209 – 259	$4/7$
260 – 262	$5/7$

14.2.7 Liability for other children under a court order

If the non-resident parent is able to pay child maintenance for another child under a court order, and an application to the CSA for that child cannot be made:

- do the calculation as if the number of qualifying children included the child who gets money under the order;
- divide the result by the total number of children;
- the CSA liability is the sum apportioned to the qualifying children.

14.3 VARIATIONS

1. Replace the old departure directions. Variations can increase or decrease payments to be made.
2. Secretary of State must consider whether:
   - a variation would result in a relevant person ceasing full-time employment;
   - the payer is having to pay under a court order made before the maintenance calculation;
   - (for special expenses variations only) financial arrangements could have been made to enable the expense to be paid without variation;
   - (for special expenses only) the non-resident parent pays expenses other than for everyday essential requirements.
3. Secretary of State cannot take into account:
   - the fact that a conception was unplanned;
   - the responsibility for breakdown in relationships;
   - the existence of a new relationship;
   - contact arrangements;
   - income or assets of any other person (except a partner);
   - failure to make payments other than the person with care and non-residential parent.

14.3.1 Variation for special expenses

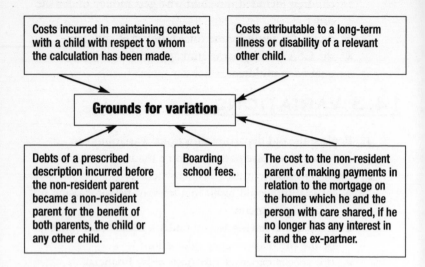

1. To get a variation with income of £200 plus, expenses must be £15 or more. For income below £200 expenses need to be £10 or more.
2. Contact costs must be part of a set pattern and may include:
   - travel tickets;
   - fuel;
   - taxi fare where needed for child with disability/long-term illness;
   - car hire (if less than public transport);
   - if overnight contact or two consecutive days and return journey impracticable, accommodation;
   - minor incidental costs, e.g. breakfast.
3. Expenses are calculated as a weekly average over 12 months.
4. Contact costs cannot be claimed for time when there is a reduction for shared care.
5. Expenses for disability may include personal attendance, mobility, domestic help, medical aids and diet.

6. Prior debts exclude gambling debts, fines, credit card debts, unpaid legal costs from separation or divorce, loans other than from a qualifying lender.

7. Payment of a debt cannot constitute a special expense where the non-resident parent has taken responsibility for the debt as part of a financial settlement with the person with care, or by a court order.

8. For claims for a mortgage, the following conditions must be met:
   - The mortgage or loan was taken out to purchase or improve a property by a person other than the non-resident parent.
   - Payments do not apply to a debt incurred by the non-resident parent.
   - Property must have been the home of the non-resident parent and person with care when they were a couple, and remains the home of the child and the person with care.
   - The non-resident parent must not have any legal or equitable interest in the property, and no charge or right to have a charge over it.

9. For school fees only, the non-educational part of the fees may be claimed. If the fees are not itemised then the Child Support Agency will determine the allowable proportion up to 35% of the total fees.

10. A school fees claim cannot reduce the net income of the payer by more than 50%.

14.3.2 Variation on the basis of assets

CSA may take into account capital assets of the payer which total over £65,000.

14.3.3 Variation for other income

CSA may vary a calculation where:

- The nil or flat rate applies, but the non-resident parent does, in fact, have an income, e.g. a student with an income.
- The non-resident parent can control his income and has unreasonably reduced it.
- Secretary of State may make an interim decision, i.e. a decision on the normal rules without regard to a variation application where there is not yet enough information to deal with the variation application.
- If an interim decision is made, a 'regular payments condition' can be imposed which is to be complied with before the variation is allowed.
- Secretary of State can agree or not agree a variation, or he can refer it to an appeal tribunal.

14.3.4 The effect of a variation

1. For special expenses, the weekly amount of the expenses are deducted from the net weekly income.
2. For additional assets, the net weekly income is increased by the extra amount to be taken into account.

14.4 REVISIONS, SUPERCESSIONS AND APPEALS

14.4.1 Revisions

1. Revisions exist to correct official mistakes or factual errors.
2. Revisions requested within one month can be done on any ground except changes of circumstances after the decision was made.

3. Revisions requested after one month will be allowed if the error resulted from an official error or a mistake, or if ignorance of a fact has led to an assessment more favourable to the claimant than would otherwise have been the case.

4. They can be applied for by parent with care, non-resident parent or the CSA.

5. An application for a revision out of time can be made within 13 months of the decision. The test is whether the time extension is reasonable.

6. Revisions cannot ever be based on ignorance or misunderstanding of the law.

14.4.2 Supercessions

1. Supercessions deal with changes of circumstances, or anticipated changes of circumstances, including changes in benefit payments.

2. These are available where:
   - there has been a change of circumstances;
   - there has been a mistake or ignorance in relation to a fact.

3. In either case, the Secretary of State must be satisfied that the change of circumstances was relevant, or that the fact was material.

4. Changes comprising a reduction in the payer's income must be of more than 5%.

5. The supercession is backdated for existing changes of circumstances. For anticipated changes, the decision applies at the time of the change.

14.4.3 Appeals

1. Appeals lie to the Appeal Tribunal.

2. Any person with care or non-resident parent (or the child in Scotland) may appeal:

- a maintenance calculation;
- default or interim maintenance calculation;
- a supercession;
- a revision of any of those decisions;
- a refusal to make a maintenance calculation;
- a reduced benefit direction.

3. No grounds for appeal are specified in the CSA 1991, but the tribunal applies the same law, so appeals are likely to be based on mistakes of fact or law or the exercise of discretion in variation applications.

4. The appeal must be made within one month of the decision, with an extra 14 days given where the tribunal requests written reasons for the appeal. A set form need not be used.

5. The tribunal cannot take into account a change of circumstances of law.

6. Appeal from the tribunal is to the Child Support Commissioner, with leave from the tribunal chair or the Commisisoner. From there it goes to the Court of Appeal.

CHAPTER 15

FINANCIAL APPLICATIONS UNDER SCHED 1 OF THE CHILDREN ACT 1989

15.1 TO WHOM DO THE PROVISIONS APPLY?

1. Applications may be made by a parent, a guardian or special guardian of a child, or by any person who has a residence order for the child.
2. Orders can be against either parent of a child.
3. The parents of the child must be living in separate households.
4. The definition of parents includes step-parents if the child is a 'child of the family'.
5. The court may make a Sched 1 order of its own volition when making or revoking a residence order.
6. Orders cannot be made against a guardian.

15.2 THE AVAILABLE ORDERS

Periodic payments, either direct to the child or to the applicant, for the benefit of the child for such a term as the order specifies.	Secured periodic payments, either direct to the child or to the applicant, for the benefit of the child for such a term as the order specifies.	Lump sum to the child or the applicant, for the benefit of the child.

The available orders for children under 18

An order making a settlement of property to which the parent is entitled, for the benefit of the child.	The transfer of property owned by the parent(s), direct to the child or to the applicant, for the benefit of the child.	The alteration of a maintenance agreement made between the parties in writing.

1. Periodic payments are only available where the Child Support Agency does not have jurisdiction. In cases where the CSA has been invoked, the court may only deal with a particular capital need of a child, and not as capitalised day-to-day maintenance (*Phillips v Peace* [1996] 2 FCR 237). If the CSA has not been used, the court's powers to order lump sums are wider (*V v V (Child maintenance)* [2001] 2 FLR 799).

2. Orders for periodic payments or secured periodic payment may be varied.

3. Lump sum orders may be for expenses incurred for maintaining the child before the order was made. Such cases demand consideration of the parties' capital assets (*Re C (a minor) (Financial Provision: Lump Sum Order)* [1994] 2 FLR 1122).

4. They may be payable by instalments which can be varied.

5. In the Family Proceedings Court, lump sums cannot exceed £1000.

6. A lump sum order may be made when periodic payments are discharged.

7. If the child has not reached the age of 18, further periodic or lump sum orders can be made after the original order, but there may only be one order per parent for a settlement or transfer of property.

8. Lump sums can be ordered to purchase a house for a child to live in, to be settled on trust until the child reaches 18 or the end of full-time education (*J v C (child: financial provision)* [1998] 3 FCR 79).

9. The court can make orders where there is no application if it is making, varying or discharging a residence order or a special guardianship order.

10. Orders may be made for children over 18 if:
    - the applicant child is, will be or (if an order is made) would be receiving instruction at an educational establishment or undergoing training for a trade,

profession or vocation, whether or not while in gainful employment;

● there are special circumstances.

11. Children over 18 may receive periodic payments or lump sums only.

12. No such order can be made where there was a maintenance order in force for the child when they were under 16.

13. Lump sum and property adjustment orders should not ordinarily be made to provide benefits for a child after he has attained his independence (*A v A (a minor: financial provision)* [1994] 1 FCR 883).

14. The court has the power to make interim orders for periodic payments or secured payments.

15. Orders for secured or unsecured periodic payments can be made in favour of a child who lives out of England and Wales with their parent, guardian or special guardian, or under a residence order and the paying parent is in the jurisdiction.

15.3 DURATION OF ORDERS

1. Orders may be backdated to the date of application.

2. They may not extend beyond the child's seventeenth birthday unless the court thinks that it is right in the circumstances to specify a later date.

3. That later date must be no later than the child's eighteenth birthday, unless the child is or would be in education or training or there are special circumstances.

4. Periodic payments cease:
   ● on the death of the recipient;
   ● if the paying and recipient parents live together again for six months.

5. Secured periodic payments do not automatically end on the death of the payer, and applications to vary them may be made, including by the dead parent's personal representatives.

15.4 RELEVANT FACTORS

1. In each case the court must consider:
   - the income, earning capacity, property and other financial resources which the parents, mother and father and applicant has or is likely to have in the foreseeable future;
   - the financial needs, obligations and responsibilities which the parents, mother and father and applicant has or is likely to have in the foreseeable future;
   - the financial needs of the child;
   - the income, earning capacity (if any), property and other financial resources of the child;
   - any physical or mental disability of the child;
   - the manner in which the child was being, or was expected to be, educated or trained.
2. Where the application is against a 'parent' who is not the mother or father of the child the court should also consider:
   - whether that person has assumed responsibility for the maintenance of the child and, if so, the extent to which and basis on which he assumed that responsibility, and the length of the period during which he met that responsibility;
   - whether he did so knowing that the child was not his child;
   - the liability of any other person to maintain the child.
3. The welfare of the child is one of the considerations, but not the paramount or even first consideration (*J v C (child: financial provision)* [1998] 3 FCR 79).
4. Maintenance for a child can properly include an allowance for the parent with care *(A v A (a minor: financial provision)* [1994] 1 FLR 657).
5. In the case of a lottery winner, it was said that the child is entitled to be brought up in circumstances which bear some sort of relationship with the father's current resources

and the father's present standard of living. The fact that such riches as they have came after the break up of the relationship cannot affect that (*J v C* [1998] 3 FCR 79).

6. In *Re P (A child)* [2003] EWCA Civ 837, the House of Lords confirmed that a child is entitled to be brought up in circumstances which bear some resemblance to the father's standard of living, but the mother is not entitled to save money from the child's maintenance for her own future.

7. It is not possible to use Sched 1 to get interim payments towards legal fees (*W v J (Child: variation of Financial Provision)* [2004] 2 FLR 300).

15.5 VARIATION APPLICATIONS

1. The court will look at all the circumstances afresh, having regard to changes of circumstances since the last order was made.

2. Orders may be suspended temporarily and revived.

3. An order varying periodic payments may be made by the child if they are now over 16.

4. In the event of an order ending on or after the child's sixteenth birthday, but before they are 18, the child may apply for the order to be revived. The power to revive is dependant on the child being in full-time education or training, or the existence of special circumstances.

INDEX